The Reminiscences

of

Captain Joseph J. Rochefort

U. S. Navy (Retired)

U. S. Naval Institute

Annapolis, Maryland

1983

Preface to Original Version

This manuscript is the result of a series of tape-recorded interviews with Captain Joseph J. Rochefort, U. S. Navy, Retired, in Redondo Beach, California during 1969. These interviews were conducted by Commander Etta-Belle Kitchen, U. S. Navy, Retired, for the Oral History Office in the U. S. Naval Institute.

Only minor emendations and corrections have been made to the manuscript. The reader is asked therefore to bear in mind the fact that he is reading a transcript of the spoken word rather than the written word.

John T. Mason, Jr.
Director of Oral History
U.S. Naval Institute
1970

Preface to Revised Version

The original version of Captain Rochefort's oral history was completed in 1970 and added to the Naval Institute collection at that point. In late 1971, the Naval Security Group Command in Washington became aware of the memoir and sent a representative to Annapolis to examine the Naval Institute's copy of the bound volume of the Rochefort transcripts. Based on this examination, the Director of Naval Intelligence in December of that year requested that the bound volume and the interview tapes be turned over to Naval Intelligence, a request which was complied with. In March 1973, Commander Naval Intelligence Command informed the Naval Institute that Captain Rochefort's oral history had been reviewed by the National Security Agency and deemed to contain material bearing the classification of secret. Accordingly, the Naval Institute's copy was not returned, and shortly thereafter the copy of the transcript held by the Naval History Division was also turned over to the Naval Security Group Command. The Naval Security Group Command still has possession of the Naval Institute's original, unmarked version of the transcript.

On 29 December 1982, the National Security Agency released to the Naval Institute a declassified version of Captain Rochefort's oral history transcript. This version contains probably 95% or more of the material in the original. The transcript released by the National Security Agency has now been retyped by the

Naval Institute with asterisks used to show the location and length of deletions which were made from the original. In the retyping process, a series of footnotes has been added for the benefit of readers, and a new, more thorough index has been compiled by Ms. Susan Sweeney of the Naval Institute staff.

Captain Rochefort's oral history will be of particular interest to those studying U.S. Navy cryptanalysis during World War II. Rochefort was one of the real pioneers in the field, getting into it in the mid-1920s, shortly after Lieutenant Commander Laurance Safford had set up the Navy codebreaking section in Washington. Rochefort describes his career as a line officer in which shipboard and staff assignments were predominant and codebreaking something of a sideline. Because of his service in these operational billets, he felt he had an edge on those who were merely codebreaking technicians.

Rochefort was not able to predict the surprise Japanese attack on Pearl Harbor in December 1941 and blamed himself for that, even though he was being much harsher on himself than others were. He explained simply that an intelligence officer's job is to tell his commander in chief today what the enemy is going to do tomorrow, and he had been unable to do that. Whether to blame or not, Rochefort more than redeemed himself in the months that followed by heading up the section which broke Japanese messages concerning the upcoming battles of the Coral Sea and Midway. Working with Lieutenant Commander Edwin T. Layton, the Pacific Fleet intelligence officer, Rochefort provided information which enabled the Navy to have its forces in the right places at the right times.

Unfortunately, controversy followed over who should get credit for the codebreaking aspect of the Midway victory, and Rochefort moved through a series of jobs which removed him from his basement room at Pearl Harbor where the men under his leadership had been so successful. This memoir is highlighted by its descriptions of the atmosphere of that room and its various occupants. Later the account tells of Rochefort's continuing work in intelligence, including some after-the-fact cryptanalysis which was used for the purpose of strategic intelligence. Through it all, one gets a feeling for the character and personality of a man who contributed much to the Navy's victory in the Pacific in World War II.

                                          Paul Stillwell
                                          Director of Oral History
                                          U.S. Naval Institute
                                          August 1983

DECLARATION OF TRUST

The undersigned does hereby appoint and designate as his (her) Trustee herein, the Secretary-Treasurer and Publisher of the United States Naval Institute to perform and discharge the following duties, powers, and privileges in connection with the possession and use of a certain taped interview between the undersigned and the Oral History Department of the United States Naval Institute.

1. Classification of Transcript.

(X)a. If classified OPEN, the transcript(s) may be read or the recording(s) audited by the qualified personnel upon presentation of proper credentials, as determined by the Secretary-Treasurer of the U. S. Naval Institute.

( )b. If classified PERMISSION REQUIRED TO CITE OR QUOTE, the user will be required to obtain permission in writing from the interviewee prior to quoting or citing from either the transcript(s) or the recording(s).

( )c. If classified PERMISSION REQUIRED, permission must be obtained in writing from the interviewee before the transcribed interview(s) can be examined or the tape recording(s) audited.

( )d. If classified CLOSED, the transcribed interview(s) and the tape recording(s) will be sealed until a time specified by the interviewee. This may be until the death of the interviewee or for any specified number of years.

2. It is expressly understood that in giving this authorization, I am in no way precluded from placing such restrictions as I may desire upon use of the interview at any time during my lifetime, nor does this authorization in any way affect my rights to the copyright of my literary expressions that may be contained in the interview.

Witness my hand and seal this 7th day of July 1970

I hereby accept and consent to the foregoing Declaration of Trust and the powers therein conferred upon me as Trustee:

CAPTAIN JOSEPH J. ROCHEFORT
U. S. NAVY, RETIRED

Joseph John Rochefort was born in Dayton, Ohio, on May 12, 1898, son of Francis J. and Ellen (Spearman) Rochefort. He attended St. Vincent's School (Loyola of Los Angeles), California, and on April 20, 1918, during World War I, enlisted in the U. S. Naval Reserve Force. He was promoted to Machinist on March 17, 1919, and was commissioned Ensign on June 5, 1919. Transferred to the U. S. Navy in that rank (temporary) on June 15, 1919, he subsequently advanced in rank, attaining that of Captain, to date from October 6, 1943. On January 1, 1947 he was transferred to the Retired list of the U. S. Navy.

Following his enlistment in the U. S. Naval Reserve Force in April 1918, he served throughout the World War I period in an enlisted capacity. In March 1919 he reported on board the USS Koningen Der Nederlanden for instruction in connection with the Navy Steam Engineering School, and after brief duty with the Naval Auxiliary Reserve, and in the Office of the District Supervisor, Naval Overseas Transportation Service, in New York, New York, he was relieved in June 1919, of active duty.

Recalled to active duty the following October, he had consecutive duty in the USS Cuyama, the USS Cardinal, and USS Stansbury and the USS Charleston until June 1922 when he rejoined the USS Cuyama. Transferred to the USS Arizona in December 1924, he served in that battleship until September 1925. The next month he became Officer in Charge of the Cryptographic Section, Office of Naval Communications, Navy Department, serving as such until September 1927.

Returning to sea, he was Executive Officer of the USS Macdonough from September 1927 until August 1929 and in September was ordered to the American Embassy, Tokyo, Japan, for instruction in the Japanese language. In October 1932 he returned to the United States, where he had duty in the Office of Naval Intelligence, Navy Department.

He joined the USS Maryland in March 1933 and in May of that year became Assistant Operations Officer on the staff of Commander Battle Force, United States Fleet, USS California flagship. He continued to serve in that capacity until June 1934, when he transferred to the staff of the Commander in Chief of the United States Fleet. Detached from that assignment in June 1936, he next had duty at Headquarters, Eleventh Naval District, San Diego, California, for the two succeeding years. In June 1938 he reported as Navigator on board the USS New Orleans, and from September 1939 until May 1941 had duty on the staff of the Commander Scouting Force, Pacific Fleet, USS Indianapolis, flagship.

In June 1941 he reported as Officer in Charge of the Combat Intelligence Unit, Pacific Ocean Areas, with headquarters in the Fourteenth Naval District, Pearl Harbor, Territory of Hawaii. He was serving in that capacity when the Japanese attacked the Naval Base at Pearl Harbor, December 7, 1941. In October 1942 he was ordered to duty at Headquarters, Western Sea Frontier, San Francisco, California, and in June 1943 he was assigned to Floating Drydock Training Center, Tiburon, California, where he was in charge of fitting out the USS ABSD No. 2. He assumed command of that floating dry dock upon her commissioning, August 14, 1943.

He again had duty in the Office of Naval Intelligence, Office of the Chief of Naval Operations from April 1944 until September 1946. For services in that assignment during World War II, he was awarded the Legion of Merit and is entitled to the Ribbon for, and a facsimile of the Navy Unit Commendation awarded the United States Naval Communication Intelligence Organization. The citations follow in part:

Legion of Merit: "For exceptionally meritorious conduct... while attached to the Division of Naval Communications, from December 7, 1941, to September 2, 1945...Captain Rochefort rendered invaluable assistance in carrying out the vital operations of the Division of Naval Communications during a critical period in the history of our country. By his tireless efforts, outstanding professional ability and conscientious devotion to the fulfillment of an exacting assignment, he contributed materially to the successful prosecution of the war..."

Navy Unit Commendation: "For distinguished service...in support of military operations during the period from December 7, 1941, to September 2, 1945. By untiring self sacrificing devotion to duty, the members of the United States Naval Communication Intelligence Organization have rendered service vital to operations in all fields of combat and have contributed inestimably to the successful prosecution of the war..."

Following duty in connection with General Court Martial at the Naval Base, Terminal Island, San Pedro, California (September-October 1946), he was transferred to the Retired List of the U. S. Navy, effective January 1, 1947.

Ordered into active military service, he reported in October 1950 as a member of the Evaluation Group, staff, Commander in Chief, U. S. Pacific Fleet. He remained in that capacity until May 1951 and the next month was assigned duty in connection with the analysis of naval engagements during World War II, on the staff of the President of the Naval War College, Newport, Rhode Island. On March 2, 1953 he was relieved of all active duty.

In addition to the Legion of Merit and the Navy Unit Commendation Ribbon, Captain Rochefort had the Victory Medal (World War I enlisted service); the American Defense Service Medal, Fleet Clasp; the American Campaign Medal; the Asiatic-Pacific Campaign Medal with one star; the World War II Victory Medal; and the National Defense Service Medal.

He was married to the former Fay Aery of Los Angeles, and they had two children, Joseph J. Rochefort, Jr., and Janet Fay Rochefort. Captain Rochefort died at Torrance, California, 20 July 1976.

Interview No. 1 with Captain Joseph J. Rochefort, U.S. Navy(Retired

Place: Captain Rochefort's home at 429 Via la Soledad,
         Redondo Beach, California

Date: 14 August 1969

Subject: Biography

Interviewer: Commander Etta-Belle Kitchen, U.S. Navy(Retired)

Q: Good morning, Captain Rochefort. I notice from your biography that you attended St. Vincent's School which is now Loyola in Los Angeles.

Captain Rochefort: That is correct.

Q: What subjects did you take there? And the reason I'm asking that question is that in your later career you did so many things that were of a genius character that I'm wondering what you might have done or what courses you might have taken that would have prepared you for this.

Captain Rochefort: St. Vincent's, as I recall, was the predecessor of Loyola, but when I attended there I attended in the grammar school group and I think the seventh and eighth grades. I did not continue on. Rather than that, I went to Polytechnic High School, which was a public high school in Los Angeles. After attending there approximately four years, I enlisted in the Navy as a naval reserve and was very quickly sent to officers' training school.

Q: How did you happen to enlist in the Navy?

Captain Rochefort: Because of the spirit of the times, I would gather. Everybody was more or less patriotic--a distinction from 1968 or '69. When some of my friends enlisted, we all went down and all enlisted. This was either in late 1917 or early 1918.

Q: I have the date of April 20th.

Rochefort: 1918?

Q: Yes, sir.

Captain Rochefort: That's probably the time then that I was actually called into the active duty. That could very well have been. I think we all went down and enlisted about the end of '17 or possibly early '18.

Q: What made you choose the Navy?

Captain Rochefort: I wanted to be an aviator, a naval aviator. I had a very high regard for these people, which was, of course, a result of the newspapers, but I never pursued that. And then, when I was called to active duty in San Pedro, shortly after that I was sent to New York where I was enrolled at Stevens Institute of Technology in an engineering class. I graduated from that in early 1919, and was then ordered as an ensign to active duty on the Cuyama. From there I just progressed in a normal way.

Q: You served in several ships then in 1919 up to 1924, didn't you?

Captain Rochefort: Yes, I served on a minesweeper, a destroyer and the Cuyama.

Q: Was that Cuyama?

Captain Rochefort: Cuyama.

Q: That was the tanker?

Captain Rochefort: That was the oiler or the tanker. We called them tankers then.

Rochefort - 4

Q: You started in it, then went on several ships and then came back to her, didn't you?

Captain Rochefort: Yes, I served two tours on the Cuyama.

Q: What were you doing? Or what were the ships doing all those years?

Captain Rochefort: We were on the West Coast. The fleet had just come to the West Coast. When I say "the fleet," I mean the battleships, cruisers, and the larger ships. They came to the West Coast in 1919, and I joined the Cuyama at that time.

Q: My information says that after the New York episode you went to inactive duty for a few months.

Captain Rochefort: For a few months, yes.

Q: What was the occasion for that?

Captain Rochefort: I don't know. That was probably when we were placed on the inactive list, and then shortly after that, oh, I would say around the middle of 1919, then I was ordered back to active duty. This was to the tanker and after serving on there about a year, then

Rochefort - 5

I was ordered to a minesweeper, all this being engineering duty. Then I was ordered to a destroyer as engineering officer. The destroyer was the Stansbury--as engineering officer--and when the Stansbury was put out of commission, I was ordered back to the Cuyama. And from there I was ordered to the Arizona.

Q: What did you do on the Arizona?

Captain Rochefort: I was the watch and division officer with the A Division, A being the auxiliary division. That was about in 1924.

Q: December 1924 to September '25, I have.

Captain Rochefort: That is probably correct. While serving on the Cuyama, one of my executive officers was named Commander Jersey, and he and I had several things in common.* One was bridge, the other being that I liked to work crossword puzzles, which were just coming into style. He remembered this, and when he was ordered to the Navy Department, he asked me if I would care to come to the Navy Department on temporary duty in connection with preparing codes and ciphers. It was then that I was introduced to cryptanalysis.

----
*Lieutenant Commander Chester C. Jersey, USN.

Q: I wanted to get to that, because to me that's where your career is so exciting, but I was wondering what happened to your aviation duty?

Captain Rochefort: As I grew up, I forgot that. I gave that up.

Q: You never tried for it after you...

Captain Rochefort: No, I never tried for it then. Then on my first temporary duty in Washington I was a student at a class in cryptanalysis and when the officer in charge, who by the way was Lieutenant Commander Safford,* was due for sea duty, I was ordered to relieve the officer in charge.

Q: That was what I was so interested in because when you read a biography it just says he went from sea duty after all these various ships and became officer in charge of the Cryptographic Section in the Office of Naval Communications, Navy Department, Washington, D.C., and my questions were loaded with what had you been doing in the background to make this assignment possible?

----

*Lieutenant Commander Laurance F. Safford, who many years later became a key figure in the controversial "winds" messages associated with the Japanese attack on Pearl Harbor.

Rochefort - 7

Captain Rochefort: Well, as I said, I was probably ordered to the Navy Department for temporary duty because of Commander Jersey's recommendation.

Q: Was that because you were good at crossword puzzles?

Captain Rochefort: Probably, and he liked my way of playing bridge with him. Auction bridge was just disappearing then into contract bridge. Contract bridge came to the fore. It was probably because of that. Then when I completed the six months' or so course with Commander Safford in charge of the section, Commander Safford became due for sea duty, and they ordered me as his relief as the officer in charge.

Q: What did they teach you in the course? He was the teacher?

Captain Rochefort: Yes, he was the actual teacher, but there were no formal education processes at all. They would just turn over maybe several messages and see which one of us could solve them quickest.

Q: How did you know how to do that?

Captain Rochefort: There was a book as I recall--at about

this time Bill Friedman, who was in charge of the Army part of this same organization, had written a book called The Elements of Cryptanalysis and this was really our bible; this was our reference book. We would study that and then attempt to solve these little cryptograms or ciphers that Commander Safford would prepare for us.

Q: They weren't real messages, they were just play-like?

Captain Rochefort: No, they were just developed to give you a knowledge of all the various systems that had been used in the past, such as playfair, vigenere table.

Q: What kind of a table?

Captain Rochefort: Vigenere.

Q: What does that mean?

Captain Rochefort: It was a table developed by a man named Vigenere back 100 or 200 years ago. It was very helpful. So we got the principles of cryptanalysis from this book of Bill Friedman. Then after that we were more or less on our own.

Q: I take it then from that comment that the Army was

earlier in the field of cryptanalysis than the Navy?

Captain Rochefort: Yes, they were. The Army was extremely fortunate in having Mr. Friedman. He might be called a modern-day father of cryptanalysis as far as we were concerned in the United States. He has my greatest respect. I would say that he was undoubtedly the best in the world at that time.

Q: Is he still living?

Captain Rochefort: He is still living, but he had one nervous breakdown that I know of, and I would say that Bill is probably pretty well burned out at the present time.*

Q: I know that in Farago's book he says that in October of 1925 another pioneer in American cryptanalysis transferred from the Arizona to the Cryptographic Section in the Navy Department, that you had made your way up through the ranks and you were an expert cryptographer regarded as the Navy's best and a Japanese linguist destined to

---

*Friedman died on 2 November 1969, less than three months after this interview was conducted. For his biography, see Ronald Clark's The Man Who Broke Purple: The Life of Colonel William Friedman, Who Deciphered the Japanese Code In World War II (Boston: Little, Brown and Company, 1977).

go far in the communications intelligence.*

Captain Rochefort: That's a slight exaggeration, I would say. In the first place I didn't study the Japanese language until 1929 to 1932. The policy of the Navy Department at that time was to order to Japan usually one or two naval officers, or sometimes Marines, to Japan, attached to the embassy for the purpose of studying and learning the Japanese language.

Q: So his statement about your being a Japanese linguist in 1925 was slightly overstated.

Captain Rochefort: That was not true.

Q: Were you in the early days then--can you describe the Navy's attempt in the early days to develop cryptographic work?

Captain Rochefort: Well, actually I don't think it would be an exaggeration to say that when Safford was ordered to the Navy Department to establish this cryptographic section, it was initially for the purpose of improving our own systems, our own crypto systems. Then in order to do this, of course, it became very apparent to Safford

---
*Ladislas Farago, The Broken Seal: The Story of "Operation Magic" and the Pearl Harbor Disaster (New York: Random House, 1967).

that a knowledge of worldwide systems in use by, say, the British, the French or the Japanese or anyone else, would be very valuable. So he sort of drifted into a study of other systems and while still making every effort to improve our own systems which were not very good at that time. He also was attacking other systems being used by other powers.

Q: In an attempt to interpret them, to decipher them?

Captain Rochefort: Yes, an attempt to interpret them, primarily at least, first for the purpose of finding out what other countries were doing in order then to improve our own system.

Q: What was Safford's background that he became assigned? Was he the first man, would you say, in the Navy?

Captain Rochefort: Yes, Safford really started this whole organization say roughly from '23 to '25 and then I followed him from '25 to '27.

Q: I wonder, do you know what made him start it? What caused him to be interested in it?

Captain Rochefort: Strangely enough, maybe the best

answer here would be if you ask a mountain climber why does he climb a certain mountain, he'll tell you because it's there. Well, why does a cryptanalyst attempt to solve some code of cipher systems?

Q: I mean, I wonder how he happened to get into or be interested in cryptanalysis at all.

Captain Rochefort: Because here was a message or a series of messages which didn't make sense to anybody, and this was a challenge.

Q: Was he then in communications?

Captain Rochefort: Yes, this was what he knew. These things just present a challenge, and a true cryptanalyst will never give up until he has solved this particular system. A true cryptanalyst, incidentally, generally is not involved in subsequent use of this at all. He's what you would call a technician who will solve a system just for the sake of solving the system. But he doesn't usually apply the results to any operation or need or purpose or anything else. This would be a true cryptanalyst. This would be Safford.

Q: So he really did it just for the love of doing it.

Captain Rochefort: Yes, it, as I said, presents a challenge to anybody. Actually, nearly all cryptanalysts are somewhat the same. Well, let me put it this way. If you desire to be a real great cryptanalyst, being a little bit nuts helps. A cryptanalyst from those that I have observed is usually an odd character.

Q: Isn't that true of most any genius?

Captain Rochefort: Yes, it is. Actually people like Safford, maybe Dyer, are people who will not generally conform to the accepted ideas.* These are regarding clothes or actions or anything of that nature, and this always helps. But, by the same token, these people who have this ability require generally somebody over them to keep them on the right track.

Q: Yes, I suppose that's true.

Captain Rochefort: I've often said it is not necessary to be crazy to be a cryptanalyst, but it always helps.

Q: Well, you were in charge of the Cryptographic Section, however.

----

*Thomas H. Dyer. As a lieutenant commander, Dyer served in Rochefort's code-breaking unit at Pearl Harbor during the early part of World War II.

Captain Rochefort: That's true. I like to consider myself as the exception; maybe I'm not.

Q: I suspect you are, because you apparently were able to do both of those things to be the Navy's outstanding cryptanalyst, cryptographer, and also you were in charge on a number of occasions of the units.

Captain Rochefort: Well, let's go back just a little bit. When I first relieved Safford in Washington, the organization consisted of the officer in charge, one cryptanalyst, and one helper, one assistant, who had no particular abilities, and that was it. Under that organization we solved the first Japanese major naval cipher system with those people.

Q: What was that called?

Rochefort: We merely called it number one ourselves, just among ourselves, because we didn't know what it was. We could read the messages.

Q: How could you read Japanese messages without knowing Japanese?

Captain Rochefort: It's not necessary to know a language,

but it is necessary to know the mechanics of the language. For example, let's say the grammar. In our system, of course, we know that "q" is invariably followed by "u." We know this and quite a few other things. We know too that going from the plural of, say, the word "carry," the plural of "carry" has "ies" on the end. You know this. This is what I call the mechanics. You should have a knowledge of the mechanics of any national system that you are trying to solve, but you don't necessarily have to know the language itself.

Q: Did you have a dictionary?

Captain Rochefort: I was coming to that. The dictionary is the solution of it. If you have a dictionary--we had one or two, I think, of the Japanese dictionaries--and this, of course, is a must. This is what is required, but in order to solve a system, particularly the systems in use in those times, you merely had to know that it was very helpful to have a general idea of what they're talking about, such as, time of war and not time of war, peacetime. But at this particular time, it was very helpful to us, as I remember, because the messages were dealing with giving the Japanese assistance as a result of the 1923 earthquake.

Q: Oh, I see. Why would they put a message like that in code?

Captain Rochefort: Well, anything that was supposed to be more or less confidential or secret--this was a secret system. Like when you're talking even about, say, giving them aid, which we did, once in a while this was referred to in the naval system which would be ciphered.

Q: But these messages were in code and in Japanese, and yet the three of you were able to solve them.

Captain Rochefort: This is correct.

Q: Tell me how it makes you feel when you are working on one of these.

Captain Rochefort: It makes you feel pretty good, as a matter of fact, because you have defied these people who have attempted to use a system they thought was secure, that is, it was unreadable. It was always somewhat of a pleasure to defeat them or challenge them. This has a lot to do with cryptanalysis itself.

Q: What are your mental processes while you do it? Are you happy, frustrated, or...

Captain Rochefort: Generally, you're frustrated. I used to tell the people--we had classes when I became officer in charge. We also had classes for special purposes. These were continued spasmodically. I used to tell these people, among other things, that the solution of one of these systems which was a mechanical system using some type of apparatus--it first off involved what I call the staring process. You look at all of these messages that you have, you line them up in various ways, you write them one below the other, and you'd write them in various forms and you'd stare at them. Pretty soon you'd notice a pattern; you'd notice a definite pattern between these messages. This was the first clue. This I referred to as the staring process.

Q: Were you the first person to think of that?

Captain Rochefort: No, oh heavens no. This had probably been done for hundreds of years, the same thing.

Q: It sounds almost like a crossword puzzle when you describe it.

Captain Rochefort: Yes, actually it is. You notice a pattern that when you follow through, you say this means so-and-so; you'd run that through, and it doesn't work out. Then you'd proceed on some other effort and eventually, if you're lucky and the other fellow makes mistakes, which he invariably will, then you come up with a solution that will stand up under test, and this gives your first lead-in. This generally I think is true in most any what I would refer to as professional systems, possibly a machine, possibly by some other procedure developed.

Q: What was done with this material? You were in communications and naval intelligence. Were you part of naval intelligence then, or were you just communications?

Captain Rochefort: No. At that time, because--you see, you might think that this place should be in the Office of Naval Intelligence, but due to the fact that in order to get this material you had to have intercept stations, you had to have copies of this material, in this particular case, Japanese Navy. This would either go over the air or through the cables. We had to have a means of intercepting them. Now these intercept operators and their equipment would be furnished by the Office of Naval Communications, for example, radio operations. Now these people were under control of Communications. What is more natural than to have the Office of Naval Communications control the whole operation up to the point where you develop messages that could be read? Then, at that point, they were turned over to Naval Intelligence. This is why Communications always ran the show. It was their equipment and their personnel.

Q: Then you made the translation and interpretation. That isn't the right word; what is the proper word?

Captain Rochefort: Translation.

Q: Translation is all right? Once you've made the translation, then it went to Naval Intelligence.

Captain Rochefort: Yes. Naval Intelligence got into the act a little bit ahead of this. They got in the act, because in order to read these messages you had to have a Japanese linguist. Now the Japanese linguist came under the Office of Naval Intelligence. So from then on, it became a sort of joint effort, between the two departments. Naval Communications had the radio sets; they had the radio operators who could be trained to copy Japanese, and so on. They had the facilities for that. So they did all the intercepting.

Q: Now, to take down a message in Japanese took a special

skill as well.

Captain Rochefort: Yes, because the dots and the dashes have different meanings from our Morse code. The Japanese Morse at that time was different from ours. So when you got the three dots and a dash or something, this might mean a "k" to the average radio operator or wireless operator, but in the Japanese system of Morse, it might have another meaning. So these people had to be placed in training to read the Japanese Morse.

Q: So many skills have to go into this.

Captain Rochefort: Yes. We had trained these people before my time out there, and they would then send in the intercepted traffic. At first, they sent this in longhand, just copied it off in pencil, and then they would send in the sheets to us, and we had to transfer these over to the Japanese equivalents and then proceed from there--or numerals, as the case may be.

Q: In your first duty here in Washington, did you learn to encrypt as well as decrypt?

Captain Rochefort: Oh, yes. We could also do that. But generally because of the technicalities of the languages concerned. Actually sometimes when you saw a foreign system--sometimes when you solve a foreign system by your various procedures, you could perhaps decrypt this stuff quicker than the original intender. For example, if you have a code and then you had a double cipher on top of this--that is you'd have a code and you'd cipher that, then you'd cipher the next thing, you have what some people would call a double cipher. Then you could possibly develop a machine or a method whereby you would wind up with a code in only one cipher, you'd combine the last two ciphers into one. This can be done in some types of systems.

Q: Did you learn all of that in your first duty here?

Captain Rochefort: Yes.

Q: In six months?

Captain Rochefort: Oh, we had just an inkling of it, just an outline of it.

Q: But you were actually in the Navy's first effort.

Captain Rochefort: No, that wouldn't be fair, because Safford had laid all the groundwork.

Rochefort - 22

Q: But I mean in the unit, that Safford and you were in this first unit that the Navy ever had.

Captain Rochefort: Yes.

Q: Well, how did Intelligence treat it? Did they take it on to the Navy Department? I'll tell you why I'm asking. I read someplace that the Navy Department was keeping something so secret that they didn't even want it to go to the President, which was laughable because the whole point of it was taking it to the person who could make decisions on it. Does this ring a bell to you? Do you know what I'm talking about?

Captain Rochefort: Yes. The difficulty at that time, and I don't believe we have this now, because the senior officers are more or less--I won't say more capable--but better or more competent. They have been indoctrinated with the value of this particular type of intelligence to the point where they are very careful. But jumping this thing back about 16 years or so, say, into 1945 or '41 and '42, the senior officers were not familiar, nor did they believe in this particular type of intelligence; we can call it communications intelligence if you want to. I recall having been sent for, two or three days after Midway, by my immediate superior who was Commander of the 14th Naval District and I was told to sit down and listen. I think this was the Prime Minister of Australia who was returning to Australia from Washington, and he told us how this whole thing had been done, the intelligence at Midway. How this had been done by breaking the Japanese code. He had just come from Washington. In other words, somebody in Washington must have been talking, and this is almost impossible to stop. Anybody that's exposed to the public as much as, say, a member of the Cabinet or the President or possibly someone in the Senate who is involved in meeting the public quite a lot very often will say things which he shouldn't say. There have been quite a few instances of this.

Q: I wonder who on earth would have made this statement. Did he ever indicate who made this statement to him?

Captain Rochefort: No, because here we are dealing at the political level. We keep away from this. But what I'm trying to point out to you is that it is not necessary in some cases for the person making the final decision to even know the source of this.

Q: I can understand that.

Captain Rochefort: And naval officers, to my knowledge,

used to talk about this. During my time in Pearl Harbor, when I was officer in charge of a station there, I made it a point--I never talked about the communications intelligence or the results of it to anyone, any person other than my opposite number who was Eddie Layton, the fleet intelligence officer, or possibly to Admiral Nimitz himself.[*] I would not talk about this to anyone else.

Q: But one wonders how that kind of information would have become almost sounds like general knowledge, so that somebody coming back to Australia--of course, again he's on a high level--but still that there would have been...

Captain Rochefort: Somebody in Washington either in CominCh's office or at the White House told him.[**] And this is not good.

Q: Going back to 1925 then, I'm wondering how the officers of intelligence used the material then. Do you know?

Captain Rochefort: Yes, they would list this as an unimpeachable source, reliable source, or something like this. Just let it go at that.

---

[*] Lieutenant Commander Edwin T. Layton, USN, Pacific Fleet intelligence officer during World War II; Admiral Chester W. Nimitz, USN, Commander in Chief Pacific Fleet.
[**] CominCh--Commander in Chief U.S. Fleet, Admiral Ernest J. King, USN.

Q: But did they use it? Were they recognizing what you were doing or were they like so many, I hate to say, conservative naval officers that anything that's new, they don't want to do it, they don't want to accept it, or don't want to use it? And I'm just wondering how they reacted in those days.

Captain Rochefort: I don't think they used it properly. I don't think they used it to the fullest extent. This business of secrecy, you see, is a sort of self-defeating thing. It is useless to obtain intelligence such as you obtain by communications intelligence organization unless you use it. But at the same time, if you don't tell anybody about this, how can it be used? This is always the big problem. As long as I was in Pearl, we attempted to solve this by--I arrogated to myself the responsibility of not only furnishing this information to Admiral Nimitz through Eddie Layton, but I also tried to convey what this meant. Now this naturally met with some resistance, because prior to my deciding on this course of action these communication intelligence people merely would hand over a message or a group of messages or an estimate or something of this nature. But they did not go beyond this and I maintained, and I was successful as long as I was in Pearl, because of my special training-- you see, in addition to this communications intelligence, I had been fleet intelligence officer. I had also been assistant fleet operations officer, and for a short period of time I was fleet operations officer, so I knew both sides of the story, both sides of the picture. So in addition to giving these fragmentary messages or maybe practically complete messages which we obtained by intercept means, I would also attempt to say what this actually meant, what the results were going to be.

Q: To interpret as well as just...

Captain Rochefort: Yes, I also did this, and this caused possibly a little hostility on the part of some people. But I felt that knowing the Japanese mind and having seen the messages, which I translated myself or at least supervised the translation, I was in a better position to say what they meant than anyone else. This was my whole approach to the thing.

Q: Did you have any of that trouble on your first job when you were a much younger and very junior naval officer?

Captain Rochefort: No. Of course, then at that time I was a junior lieutenant. Then I became a senior lieutenant during my tour there from 1925 to '27. Being a junior lieutenant and a senior lieutenant, I was in no position to make any estimates unless I was asked to. Later on, of course, during the war, then I believed very strongly that I was better prepared to indicate what was in the Japanese mind than, for example, the planning people on Nimitz's staff or the operations people on Nimitz's staff. That is why we always, at any opportunity, we'd always specify what this meant, not only to the immediate business in this whole thing such as a copy of a Japanese operations order, but we also sent in judgments, and in order to accomplish this, obviously the Japanese intend to do so and so. That is where I differed from most intelligence organizations at that time.

Q: I want to pursue that when we get a little bit more chronologically to Pearl; there is no limit to what I want to know from you. What were the developments in the Navy Department's cryptographic profession in the two years you were there in Washington? I would think so much groundwork would have been laid during that time.

Captain Rochefort: No, Safford did all the groundwork. For example, from Safford I inherited the job of completing the obtaining of special typewriters, working directly through Underwood myself. This is one thing that Safford had started to be completed. So instead of writing longhand, all the operators had to do was to punch the keys. This was started by Safford. The expansion of the intercept system by opening new intercept stations—this was done by Safford. He started all this whole thing, and he would be considered then the father of this whole thing which developed into the communications intelligence organization.

Q: What did the typewriters do?

Captain Rochefort: The operators were trained to copy directly from the Japanese and instead of coming out with English, they would come out with Japanese characters.

Q: That could then be interpreted?

Captain Rochefort: Yes, and it was a far step forward when they obtained typed material. It made the job a lot easier for our interceptor, too.

Q: And it was you, and what was the other man's name?

Captain Rochefort: Safford was the first officer in charge. I relieved Safford, and from then on we had other people to relieve each other.

Q: But there was you—you said three of you only in the office.

Captain Rochefort: Yes, we had one lady who was exceptionally good.

Q: Was that Miss Aggie?

Captain Rochefort: Miss Aggie. And then we had a man who was a sort of an assistant; you might call him a clerk. He was an ex-actor, incidentally. But he became sick during my tenure there. We had to get him relieved by another clerk.

Q: So it was just the three of you.

Captain Rochefort: That's all.

Q: And what were the intercept stations?

Captain Rochefort: Mostly Shanghai. Shanghai, and then later on we developed other stations, such as on the mainland here and in between at Pearl Harbor, you see.

Q: Tell me about Miss Aggie. I read about her in a couple of books.

Captain Rochefort: I would say that Mrs. Driscoll--I used to refer to her either as Aggie or Mrs. Driscoll, and then she was a Miss for a long time--Meyer was her name, Agnes Meyer originally. Then she became Mrs. Driscoll, but we usually referred to her as Aggie. I would say she was a first-class cryptanalyst. There was considerable competition between she and Friedman--considerable competition. She was extremely capable, very quiet, and the thing I think more and more was how she used to turn the pages on the book or dictionary--she'd do it with the rubber end of a pencil, always flipping over pages in the upper right-hand corner--that's what I always remember most about her. She was a very talented person--awfully good. I don't know where she is now.

Q: How had she learned it?

Captain Rochefort: As I recall now, she worked for the Army for a while. When I first came in contact with Mrs. Driscoll in 1925 in Washington, she was exceptionally capable, very capable. I considered her sort of a teacher to me.

Q: Is she credited with breaking any particular Japanese code?

Captain Rochefort: I would say she was mostly responsible for the first one we solved while I was in charge. She deserves all the credit for that.

Q: How many hours would she have had to work on that?

Captain Rochefort: Oh, I don't know; I would say maybe a year or so while I was there in charge. Possibly a year is what it took and that's with a lot of luck. Then we just turned it over. You see, at that time naval officers, particularly junior lieutenants and lieutenants, would only remain on shore duty for two years. You had to have that system in order to get promoted. So if you wanted to stay there, your chances of promotion would get less and less. That is why Safford only remained there during a definite period of time, probably somewhere around two or two and a half years. I would remain there two years, and my successor would remain there two years and so on, which possibly had an advantage in that we got fresh blood in there all the time. Then you get these different ideas and approaches to the same problem.

Q: But they all had to go through a training period.

Captain Rochefort: Yes, they did. Of course, gradually we would build up this very small organization, then we developed a little nucleus of people who had been in charge of one of the classes and had some special qualification.

Rochefort - 32

Q: Did they volunteer to do this, request it, or did it just happen by happenstance to get...

Captain Rochefort: You usually request them. Of course, this was rather harmful, I think, to their careers also, in that you became known as one of these nuts. Every time he goes to Washington and goes in this particular division, nobody knows what he does or anything else, so he becomes known as somewhat of a nut. And some of them were.

Q: How many people in the Navy Department knew of this section?

Captain Rochefort: Oh, I don't know, maybe in, let's say, 1930--and this is just a pure guess--maybe a couple of dozen. We kept it very quiet.

Q: That's why I was wondering how they would have known even to request it?

Captain Rochefort: Well, you might get--I think it was Mr. Kahn who said Dyer was associated with Safford on one of the fleet cruises where we were conducting some sort of a small arms shooting and training exercises which they used to do, and he talked with Safford and

Safford had him hooked.*

Q: Oh, person-to-person information then.

Captain Rochefort: Yes, person to person. There was no publicity.

Q: I read in a book about cryptanalysis written by an L.D. Smith, and he indicated the characteristics of a good intelligence man. He said a cryptanalyst possesses a quality of intellect that defies description and mystifies more average minds.

Captain Rochefort: Yes, I think that's true. I think that I'd put a little preface a little more crudely when I say that a cryptanalyst very often is the person on the verge between brilliance and being crazy. You just have to have this type of mind. You have to have considerable patience. These always help. Nowadays, of course, as time goes on, a good cryptanalyst would be probably a top-flight mathematician, among other things.

Q: And a top-flight bridge-player.

---
*David Kahn. The Codebreakers (New York: Macmillan, 1967).

Captain Rochefort: No, not necessarily that. That would help for the same reason. The difference between a good bridge player and a poor bridge player is that fellow that's going to make, let's say, ten tricks and the poor guy is going to make nine tricks out of every hand, merely because he analyzes.

Q: And he has a mathematical kind of a mind.

Captain Rochefort: Yes, he has to know what all the odds are and what the probabilities are and so on and so forth. He has to know this, and he has to be an excellent mathematician, particularly when discussing, say, machine systems; that is, systems made up around some kind of a machine.

Q: How did you learn your patience? Were you born patient?

Captain Rochefort: No, there's that constant challenge. You see a whole lot of letters and a whole lot of numerals, perhaps in the thousands or millions, and you know that there is a system in there, and there's a little key to the system that's something real simple, and you just keep after it until you finally solve it. Then you solve it and get on to something else. But it takes a particular type of mind. I know of no cryptanalyst in the Navy that has ever proceeded in a normal way on the promotion list; none of them do. Maybe this is because they become so enamored or preoccupied that they don't make very good naval officers.

Q: I'm guessing that one is born with these characteristics then.

Captain Rochefort: It's possible.

Q: You can't acquire it, can you?

Captain Rochefort: No. It take a person with certainly an analytical mind, a person who is on pretty firm ground in higher mathematics. A knowledge of the mechanics of the language involved is something very helpful. Then a persistence, just sticking with this thing day after day after day.

Q: And accuracy?

Captain Rochefort: Well, yes, his mind has got to operate logically, because he would be forever testing these various hypotheses. Could it be a code? How he would prove or disprove this right away. Then what type of a cipher, and is it a machine type, or is it something prepared by hand? That is one of these old things where you have key words and things like that. You could do the job pretty fast, and naturally the more experienced you become, the quicker becomes the process.

Q: Yardley says--is his book called The Black Room?

Captain Rochefort: The Black Chamber.*

Q: He says that breaking the Japanese code was hopeless up to his time in 1919.

Captain Rochefort: I wouldn't even compare Yardley with some of the other people. Yardley was an opportunist, and I would say that he'd be a so-so cryptanalyst.

Q: He wrote a great big thick book about it.

Captain Rochefort: I was in Japan at the time studying the language, and that occasioned considerable discussion among the Japanese.

Q: When his book came out?

Captain Rochefort: Yes. You see, Yardley had--this was just prior to what we call the Washington Conference, the Disarmament conference.

----

*Herbert O. Yardley, The American Black Chamber (Indianapolis: Bobbs-Merrill Co., 1931).

Q: That was 1923, wasn't it?

Captain Rochefort: In '21. Yardley reading some of the Japanese diplomatic systems that to the American were rather easy to solve. Those involved were the diplomatic people, foreign office people, ************************** and that class of person. They didn't have the slightest concept of security. It's sort of a standing joke that as long as a person kept a code book in his possession, it was completely unbreakable. This was and still is among a lot of people.

Q: That means that if you don't use it, it's unbreakable?

Captain Rochefort: If you don't use it, it is unbreakable or as long as you had maintained physical possession of it, the book or pamphlet or whatever you're going to use--as long as you maintained physical possession of this, no one is going to be able to solve it. This we were very insistent upon. Well, for the sake of argument...

Q: I don't really understand that.

Captain Rochefort: The diplomatic people for some strange reason believed that the code or cipher system that they had been using possibly for 20 years, possibly for 30 years, was unbreakable, provided that no book has ever been removed or compromised or no enemy has ever seen a copy of this book. This, of course, was ridiculous.

Q: You mean that's idiotic, because anyone who can decipher can decipher without the code. I see.

Captain Rochefort: I remember in one of my classes I gave them quite a large number of messages that had been sent ** dealing with the Japanese earthquake in 1923, dealing with how many board feet of lumber are being sent on, how much food was being sent on, it was just nothing. I turned over this series of messages to one of my classes, and this was encoded in a ************************************** code which is confidential. They came up with a solution real fast, no problem. But you could never convince *********************. Because I reported this, I got over to ************************** and they got quite indignant over this whole thing. They said it couldn't be, because never in their history had they lost a copy of this ****** code. Therefore, no one else could beat it. Of course, this was ridiculous.

Q: Well now, was that before you...

Rochefort - 39

Captain Rochefort: That was in Washington from '25 to '27.

Q: And you gave them samples that you had collected through the years.

Captain Rochefort: Yes, because at that time, you see...

Q: How did you approach going to ******************************

Captain Rochefort: I didn't go to ********************* because you see at that time all this traffic *********************** ** had to go over the Navy communications system so we always could copy them off.

Q: And who did you tell how easy it was to break this?

Captain Rochefort: My immediate superior, the Director of Naval Communications.

Q: And did he tell *********************?

Captain Rochefort: He told *********************** and they became, oh, a little bit indignant, would be the word.

Q: Did they do anything about it?

Captain Rochefort: No, because obviously we were interfering in their lives--we were a threat. The Navy refused to believe this. And there are still a lot of people the same way.

Q: Isn't that crazy. Well, what do you think of Mr. Yardley? You say he's only just a mediocre...

Captain Rochefort: If I met him, it was only once. I may have met him possibly through Friedman, possibly, because that would be the contact here, you see. But I don't recall anything about him. But I would say, knowing what he was doing and what he had done, he was just a so-so cryptanalyst.

Q: He's rather expansive on his own claims when he says that breaking the Japanese code was hopeless up to him.

Captain Rochefort: Yes, this, of course, doesn't make sense, because in World War I in 1918 Friedman was with the Army, and he made his mark during World War I. There is no one that could compare with Friedman, no one at all.

Rochefort - 41

Q: Did Yardley defect to the Japanese?

Captain Rochefort: No.

Q: I had the impression from someplace that he sold out, that he was paid and defected to the Japanese.

Captain Rochefort: I may have read something to that effect, but if so, then this had to be sort of an imaginary thing on his part, because from what I could gather at that time he was operating separately and distinctly from the Army and the Navy. They worked through the State Department and the Army or Navy may have contributed something, may have--I do not know. But at that time, from say '25 to '29, Yardley was working on what we called the diplomatic systems. Those were the systems that foreign officers used and state departments and people of a similar level. These are the systems that they used. The ambassadors, the counselors, that sort of thing. Now these people had nothing whatever to do with the Army or the Navy--nothing. And during my two years in Washington, I had no contacts whatever with Mr. Yardley. I knew what he was doing. This was sort of gossiped around. I also knew that the Army was doing the same thing through Friedman and that we, when we got around to it on occasion, we would do this too. But we never interchanged anything, except possibly between the Army and the Navy, because we were not about to coordinate our activities with ********************, simply because we didn't trust them. We wouldn't trust these people. I wouldn't trust them today as a matter of fact.

Q: To expand on that a bit.

Captain Rochefort: I would say during my time there we worked very closely with the Army.

Q: I mean about not trusting them, when you say you don't trust them.

Captain Rochefort: Because these people hadn't the slightest idea of security, not the slightest. Now this is just a generalization, and like all generalizations, it's false.

Q: Another exception, sure.

Captain Rochefort: To the best of my knowledge, I would never indicate anything regarding the success or failure of communications intelligence to anybody outside communications intelligence.

Q: But you think *********************** has a very

cavalier approach to security? That isn't their prime interest.

Captain Rochefort: No, they're not at all concerned. Of course, I'm not prepared to say anything about 1969 or 1968. But I'm talking now about, say, during the Twenties or possibly during the Thirties. They possibly had the best intentions. They just did not understand security and also because many of the people in the ******************** at that time would be dealing quite a bit with the foreigners. There may or may not have been cocktail parties involved and things like that. There undoubtedly were. You couldn't trust these people to keep their mouths shut, so we just didn't say anything. That was real simple. In the Navy now we kept everything to ourselves, but I don't want you to get the idea that we didn't cooperate with the Army.

Q: No, you haven't given me that idea.

Captain Rochefort: And the Army cooperated with us. But this might be done with just a wink or just a few words. There have been many instances where Friedman was very, very helpful in working on some particular type of system, without admitting that the Army and the Navy were working together. We really were at that level.

Q: What was his position in the Army?

Captain Rochefort: He was a cryptanalyst, a captain in the Army Reserve, I believe.

Q: What did they call their section?

Captain Rochefort: It was a part of G-2, but again it was run more or less by the Signal Corps. Because they had the equipment and the personnel, the same as the Navy. You might say that Friedman and I were on the technician level.

Q: You were counterparts in your respective services?

Captain Rochefort: Yes, we were more or less counterparts, except that he would remain there and I would go to sea.

Q: And he had been there before you?

Captain Rochefort: Yes. Friedman had come in the Army, as I recall, in '17.

Q: And had gone directly into this work?

Captain Rochefort: Yes, he was employed for this purpose.

Q: As an Army officer?

Captain Rochefort: Yes, as a reserve.

Q: When was the pioneer work on red machine begun? Was it during this?

Captain Rochefort: I do not know. I couldn't give you any assistance on that, because after my tour of duty there from '25 to '27, I wanted to get in the fleet. I considered myself a naval officer, and I would much prefer to have gone through the normal tours of a ship or shore duty such as a watch and division officer, head of department, executive officer and so on. So I made every effort to keep away from cryptanalysis.

Q: Oh, you did.

Captain Rochefort: Oh yes, every effort.

Q: Didn't it hurt you to leave the job?

Captain Rochefort: No, because I had ulcers as a result of this 1925 to '27.

Q: Did you? Tell me more about that, because you haven't

really given me enough of your personal feelings in here to make me realize that it had caused an ulcer.

Captain Rochefort: Well, in my particular case, oh possibly three evenings out of four, maybe more often, I would come home say at 5:00 or 5:30 or 6:00 in the evening from the Navy Department, and I would immediately have to lie down because I couldn't eat anything maybe until 8:00 or 9:00 at night. I just couldn't eat anything.

Q: The tension?

Captain Rochefort: The tension, and this is also standard among these people. As I said before, Friedman had a nervous breakdown. I think this was prior to World War II. But I made every effort to keep away from this whole thing after I left there.

Q: Was it the tension caused from concentration?

Captain Rochefort: That's what I would say. In other words, you bring your work home with you--not actually, you don't bring any books home or anything, but you bring your problems home with you. You might be carrying on a conversation with somebody, and an idea might suddenly strike you, and you'd be thinking about this rather than carrying on the conversation.

Rochefort - 47

Q: So it's in your mind all the time.

Captain Rochefort: Constantly, 24 hours out of the day.

Q: Because there was not in that period a world crisis that would have made the traffic of such critical nature, was there?

Captain Rochefort: No, there wasn't that pressure. It was merely here is a bunch of messages and I can't read them. Now what's wrong? It was this sort of a thing, you see. And this is sort of standard. You'll find peple like this who maybe go into a trance, what looks like a trance when you're talking with them, and the first thing you notice is that they are not paying any attention to you at all, and their mind is on this other problem which they brought home from the office, brought home from the Navy Department.

Q: Did you take a drink and relax?

Captain Rochefort: No, it just took me a couple or three hours to sort of unwind before I could have a meal. I don't think this is unusual, but in any event I tried to keep away from this business.

Rochefort - 48

Q: You were an awfully young man to have an ulcer.

Captain Rochefort: Yes. And then also I had some very enjoyable sea duty.

Q: Your next duty--according to my information, you were executive officer of the Macdonough for two years.

Captain Rochefort: Yes, and she was the division flagship. I spent three years on there, which was required by our then-existing rules. You had to get in your two years.

Q: And you were a lieutenant?

Captain Rochefort: I was a lieutenant.

Q: What was your job? Division officer?

Captain Rochefort: I was executive officer and navigator. In destroyers at that time, the executive officer was also the navigator and being that we were the flagship of the 36th Division, I was then navigator for the division, for six destroyers.

Q: Where did you learn that?

Captain Rochefort: Oh, just from the previous ten years.

Q: When you were on your other ships before you ever went to the cryptographic section.

Captain Rochefort: Yes.

Q: Were you happy to be back at sea?

Captain Rochefort: Very happy. It was very good duty, and I liked destroyer duty. It was very rough duty, of course, because as I recall the first year or so, my commanding officer and my captain was a Carpender. He was known as "Chips" Carpender, A.S. Carpender, and he became ComSoWesPac for a while during World War II.[*] He was a very demanding person and a marvelous naval officer, most competent; unfortunately, his requirements reached nearly perfection.

Q: Is that all?

Captain Rochefort: That was all. He merely required perfection.

---

[*] Lieutenant Commander Arthur S. Carpender, USN. In 1942-1943, as a vice admiral, he was Commander Southwest Pacific Area.

Q: Did he appreciate it when he got it?

Captain Rochefort: I don't think he ever did get it to his own satisfaction. He'd be very rough on his officers, very rough.

Q: Was he perfect in his...

Captain Rochefort: As far as I was concerned, he set a marvelous example, which his officers just couldn't meet naturally. But that training was very valuable training.

Q: Yes, I'm sure it was a wonderful experience.

Captain Rochefort: It wasn't very happy, but you can't expect a young naval officer to be happy.

Q: I'm sure you are an expert navigator, because the math and the other qualities you have certainly are required in navigation.

Captain Rochefort: Well, that reminds me of a story, a little anecdote. A fellow I knew a little later, Commander Frost--H. H. Frost--later on when I became acquainted with him, he was navigator of the California, which at that time was the flagship, and he was also writing children's books on the Navy, kids' books. He was also writing some professional papers dealing with the Navy and he was being ordered as the fleet operations officer. I asked him one time if this didn't conflict a little bit with his job as a navigator, and then Commander Frost told me, "Any fool can be a navigator."

Q: That may be true, but he may not get where he wants to go.

Captain Rochefort: That was just merely his version.

Q: That was his evaluation of a navigator.

Captain Rochefort: Being a navigator of the Battle Force flagship to him was a minor detail.

Q: I wouldn't want to have him as my navigator, would you?

Captain Rochefort: He was a very delightful man.

Q: Was he a good navigator in spite of it?

Captain Rochefort: He was a marvelous navigator. Unfortunately,

Rochefort - 52

he died very suddenly, I think while he was still commander.*
He was one of the more competent naval officers.

Q: A man of many parts.

Captain Rochefort: When he was a junior lieutenant, this fellow used to lecture at the Naval War College on the Battle of Jutland and as a junior lieutenant he was lecturing commanders and captains. We used to call him "Holloway Halstead Miscellaneous Papers Frost."

Q: How had you known him? Were you serving with him?

Captain Rochefort: Because I was in the process of moving over to the California as an assistant operations officer.

Q: And who relieved your captain? You said the first year was rough and I thought maybe he was...

Captain Rochefort: He was relieved by a fellow named Oliver Downes who was what you might call a Naval Academy type. This is, he did all of his sea duty anywhere he could get it, and then he'd do his shore duty at the Naval Academy. They called him "Pug" Downes; that was his name.

----
*Commander Holloway H. Frost, USN, died in January 1935 at the age of 45.

Rochefort - 53

Q: Did you ever regret not having gone to the Navy through the Academy?

Captain Rochefort: No. In one respect, yes. If I had gone to the Naval Academy, I would have been well-trained in things that you just don't do--that you don't get away with. For example, you don't fight City Hall. I would have had that brainwashed into me a long time ago. I didn't have that, so I would be more inclined to speak up when I should have kept my mouth shut.

Q: And you'd be an admiral now instead of a captain.

Captain Rochefort: Well, I don't know about that. That could have been true. I would have benefited considerably by my four years at the Naval Academy, had I had the opportunity, because then I am sure I would have reacted differently under certain circumstances.

Q: Did you ever find the reaction of Academy people to you--did you find them reacting negatively to you because you were not an Academy graduate?

Captain Rochefort: Yes, something like the colored people have today.

Rochefort - 54

Q: I hope not that bad.

Captain Rochefort: But this would be only by junior officers who sometimes were--what would be the expression?--gung ho for the Naval Academy. I think we've long ago gotten away from that. But I would run across those instances occasionally but never from anybody a little senior.

Q: Do you think that interfered with your promotions other than the way you have already explained it, that your attitude in certain cases might have been different?

Captain Rochefort: Yes, I would have been more diplomatic, more politic. I sometimes think if I hadn't been coddled or made a protégé of by some people, it would have been better.

Q: Will you explain that later?

Captain Rochefort: Yes, several times I would be what you might call the protégé or fair-haired boy to some admiral such as Commander in Chief or Commander Scouting Force or something like this.

Q: And when this comes, will you be sure--I'll try to remind you.

Captain Rochefort: Well, this is not good, because I would be given authority way beyond my rank, particularly when I served with Admiral Reeves, when he was ComBatFor and Commander in Chief.[*] This experience was good at that particular moment, but it didn't serve me well later on, because naturally when a younger officer is given authority beyond his position, very often it restricts him later on.

Q: It doesn't necessarily make him popular with others. Well, let's see. Your two years you found were happy on the Macdonough or at least worthwhile overall.

Captain Rochefort: Oh yes, this was excellent. Being out in the fleet and...

Q: Where was the Macdonough then, in the Pacific?

Captain Rochefort: She was part of DesRon 12, which was assigned to Commander Destroyers Battle Force.

Q: All in the Pacific.

Captain Rochefort: They used to call destroyers--these would be the old four-stackers--we used to call them

---

[*] Admiral Joseph M. Reeves, USN, Commander Battle Force and Commander in Chief U.S. Fleet in the mid-1930s.

the "light cavalry of the sea."

Q: Where was the home base--Long Beach?

Captain Rochefort: San Diego. And we were with the fleet. We were actually operating with the fleet. And by fleet, I refer to the battleships and cruisers which were up here and the carriers which were originally up here. So we were operating with what we called the Grand Fleet.

Q: What year did the carriers join the fleet--about the early Twenties? The Langley I think was '22.

Captain Rochefort: Yes, the Langley was the first one and the Sara[toga] and the Lexington.

Q: Early in the Twenties, so the carriers hadn't been in the fleet too long when you...

Captain Rochefort: No, they joined the fleet probably--I'm just guessing--in the latter part of the Twenties.

Q: Early Twenties, I think.

Captain Rochefort: It might have been earlier.

Rochefort - 57

Q: Did you wish then that you had not given up your aviation wishes?

Captain Rochefort: No, I had forgotten this.

Q: Now my next biographical note relates to your assignment in Tokyo. Was there anything between Macdonough and Tokyo that isn't...

Captain Rochefort: No, I was only about two or two and a half years, as I recall, on the Macdonough.

Q: Let's see, I have September '27 to August '29--almost exactly two years.

Captain Rochefort: Well, it might have been that.

Q: Tell me how you happened to go to the American Embassy. Now, was this your choice, or did you want to go, or did somebody just decide they were going to send you?

Captain Rochefort: I had given no thought to it at all until I received a letter from the Navy Department asking me if I would be interested in going to Japan for the purpose of learning the language.

Q: They did ask you.

Captain Rochefort: Yes. Later I found that Captain Zacharias had suggested this. I knew nothing about it whatever, and I hadn't considered the possibility, because I was married, and in those days the Navy Department disliked to send anybody out there who was married. As a matter of fact, I think there were only two of us that were married, the other fellow being Ethelbert Watts.*
And I was, I think, the only other one that was married that was sent out there.

Q: Did they send your wife with you?

Captain Rochefort: Oh yes. This was a very, very pleasant interlude, the three years out there. That was from '29 to '32.

Q: Tell me about Captain Zacharias. How did he come to recommend you?

Captain Rochefort: It probably goes back to when I was in charge of the section in Washington from '25 to '27. I had need of a translator, a Japanese translator, and I asked the Naval Intelligence if they could provide

---
*Lieutenant (junior grade) Ethelbert Watts, USN.

me with a translator for a short period of time to help us out, and they sent down Lieutenant Commander Zacharias.*
He worked with us, I guess, for a couple of months in helping us translate some messages.

Q: And how had he learned the Japanese?

Captain Rochefort: He was a Japanese language officer. He had been out in Japan earlier. He had been out in Japan I think from '21 to '24 or something like this. Then he was down in our section working with us translating, which is where he got his little bit of knowledge about cryptanalysis.

Q: That was his introduction to it?

Captain Rochefort: That was his introduction. Then he went as the Asiatic Fleet intelligence officer later on; he and I had some correspondence during that period of time when he was the Asiatic Fleet intelligence officer and I was still the officer in charge. Then apparently, I don't know whatever caused him to do it, but apparently he suggested my name to BuNav.**

---

*Lieutenant Commander Ellis M. Zacharias, USN, who later wrote the book Secret Missions: The Story of an Intelligence Officer (New York: G. P. Putnam's, 1946).

**BuNav - the Bureau of Navigation, which was in charge of Navy personnel assignments.

Rochefort - 60

Q: What was his job at that time?

Captain Rochefort: He was in the Office of Naval Intelligence. I'm just mentioning this because I think that's what happened. Zach told me anyway that he was responsible for this. Later on he told me. So, anyway, I was ordered to Japan in the fall of '29 and stayed three years.

Q: I'd like to know how you went about learning the Japanese language.

Captain Rochefort: Well, different people had different ideas. I think the policy of only sending single officers out there, bachelors, was in the belief that these people would associate more with the Japanese than the married officer would because the latter would have his family with him. I think this was probably the belief, but I never held with this at all. I don't think it was correct; I don't think it was valid. In any event, when we went out there, we were given the magnificent sum of $50 a month bonus money, extra money.

Q: Overseas pay.

Captain Rochefort: Yes. And from this then we had to

hire instructors. $50 a month.

Q: You paid the instructors?

Captain Rochefort: Yes, we paid all of our own instructors. You see, the policy at that time was that you are sent out there and attached to the embassy, which gives you a diplomatic standing and you are under the control of the naval attaché, who in turn, of course, was controlled by the ambassador. All right. So you're sent out there, and in my particular case, I remember the naval attaché told me, "Don't come down here unless you have something serious to talk about. I expect you to be out among the Japanese learning the language, and that is your only task. That's all you're out here for and you go about it. If you want to have instructors, if you want to do it on your own, if you want to travel around the countryside, this is fine. But just learn the language, and we'll give you an examination in six months and see how much you have learned."

Q: And did you know it was going to be a full three years?

Captain Rochefort: Oh yes.

Q: So you had your own choice of how you were going to learn.

Captain Rochefort: And most of us did this the same way generally. We would hire somebody who would come around perhaps for an hour a day, and we might have two of these people if we wanted. You'd have somebody come for an hour a day and somebody else come an hour a day. In my particular case, I just had one fellow come around an hour a day and this used up my $50.

Q: I was going to ask. It did cost you $50 a month.

Captain Rochefort: Yes, that came out of my own pocket. It cost me money to hire other people. I might have, say, a college graduate come around and take conversation, just conversation. This didn't cost me anything, because we went 50-50 on this. I was teaching him English, and he was teaching me Japanese. Of course, it was impossible to do this on $50 a month, but it was sufficient. We could get by.

Q: Did Mrs. Rochefort learn Japanese too?

Captain Rochefort: Well, yes, conversational Japanese. She could pick up words if she wanted to go from one place to another, if she wanted to ask questions, or things like that or pertaining to the house.

Rochefort - 63

Q: She had servants?

Captain Rochefort: Yes, we had a couple of servants which came out of our own pocket.

Q: Gee, that's hard to realize now, isn't it?

Captain Rochefort: If you wanted to learn the Japanese language, then you should be willing to pay for it.

Q: Well, but the Navy wanted you to learn it. It wasn't your idea.

Captain Rochefort: Well, that's true too. I think this is preferable to giving out all the extra money which is what they do now. If you wanted to spend money on some particular subject or something, then be my guest, but the Navy Department had no money for this.

Q: Can you describe a little bit of the way you went about learning it--that is, the complexity of the language?

Captain Rochefort: Of course, I knew most of the what they called the kata kana then from my days in Washington. Kata kana, which is the simplified way of writing and hira gana, which is the more cursive method; people call it cursive script, if you wanted to. This was instead of using the Chinese characters, you used the kata kana or the hira gana before you started in on the Chinese characters. You'd learn those. Of course, everybody did this thing a little differently. We would establish a period for an instructor to come and possibly, in my particular case, I would study for a couple of hours memorizing all the characters. And then maybe another instructor would come and then possibly I would take a walk and chat with people on the street.

Q: How many characters did you learn?

Captain Rochefort: Oh, around 3,500 or so.

Q: Is that strictly memorizing?

Captain Rochefort: Yes, to a very great extent it is. It's a strict memorization of Japanese sounds and Chinese sounds.

Q: They use Chinese symbols?

Captain Rochefort: Yes. This would be normally associated with Japanese, the Chinese characters which were taken over by the Japanese. Very often the Japanese used their own sound for this. The Chinese may call it one thing and the Japanese call it something else, a different word. But in that process, of course, you get to learn quite a bit of the Chinese language also.

Q: Did you find that extremely difficult, or did you have the kind of brain that it wasn't?

Captain Rochefort: No, not particularly. With that particular thing, it was a question of memorization mostly. No, I wouldn't call learning Japanese too difficult. We did it later on in 11 or 12 months--during the war this was. We spent three years on it. And then you were supposed to, incidentally, pick up the mores of the people themselves-- how the Japanese lived, how would they react, what did they do, and so on and so forth. You picked this up as you went along. But no, I wouldn't call it too difficult.

Q: You spoke once about knowing how the Japanese mind works--tell me, are you relating that to what you learned in this period?

Captain Rochefort: Well, you could if you paid attention. Under given circumstances, you would just about know what the Japanese reaction would be.

Q: Could you give me a for instance?

Captain Rochefort: Yes. I recall talking at some party with a fellow about my age, Japanese, and he was with Mitsui Company. His family was the Mitsui Company. Mitsui along with Mitsubishi were the two largest concerns in Japan. You might call them General Electric and General Motors or something like that. This is the time when the Japanese had become involved in Manchuria and had then gone down to Shanghai and started their operations in Shanghai. I asked this fellow, "Why did you do a thing like this because you know that you cannot defeat the Chinese."

He said, "That's right. But you're forgetting one thing. Our honor has become involved in this, and when honor becomes involved you should forget all of the realistics. That is why we went down to Shanghai. Now Caucasians and you Americans, you don't understand this at all. But we understand the Japanese. When honor is involved, we don't care about anything else." I might say that this is a little bit stupid. To become involved in a war, for example, that you know you are going to lose, why do you continue? One simple reason--honor.

Q: They didn't have any idea that they were going to lose when they went into World War II, I am sure.

Captain Rochefort: Oh sure they did. They knew they couldn't win World War II. I say "they"--I mean the people at the top level. For example, Yamamoto.* He was under no delusions whatever. But after December 7th, he knew that they were not going to win. He knew this himself.

Q: Tell me about that. Why? How?

Captain Rochefort: Because he was realistic. He had spent a couple of tours of duty over here; he'd been around the world, and he knew the Japanese were not going to defeat the United States.

Q: But wasn't he one of the men who was so adamant on going to war?

Captain Rochefort: That is correct, because he could see no other solution.

Q: To what?

Captain Rochefort: Other than going to war. To the Japanese dilemma.

Q: Of having to expand on the dilemma. You say the Japanese dilemma.

---

*Admiral Isoroku Yamamoto, Commander in Chief Japanese Combined Fleet.

Rochefort - 68

Captain Rochefort: The Japanese can't win in China. They knew this. When they started on this thing, they knew they couldn't win in China, but they had to go there for what they call honor. Then they became involved with the United States and this leads up gradually to a tightening of restrictions. For example, we had denied the Japanese money in 1941. We cut off their money. Then later on we cut off their fuel, then later on we cut off generally the trade with the Japanese.

Q: Sending them scrap iron, I remember is a particular item.

Captain Rochefort: We dropped all this off, and we were just tightening the screws on the Japanese. They could see no way of getting out of having to go to war, and, of course, the climax came in the so-called November 27 message in which we told the Japanese they could make peace in the Pacific if they did three things. This is really what we told them. If they did three things: (1) Get out of China. Now, this they could possibly have done, although it would have been awfully difficult to explain to the Japanese people. We are very sorry, we've lost two or three million troops over in China. Now we're just going to write the whole thing off and get out of China. But they might possibly have done this. They may possibly have.

Then, the second thing that we warned them about was to get rid of this tripartite pact that they had with Italy and Germany. They would have done this, because they didn't want this anyway. There was no particular problem here.

Then we tell them the third condition: to forget about this Greater East Asia Co-prosperity Sphere. Well, now how could the Japanese possibly have done this and still remain the great power? There was no way for them to go.

Q: Did we force them into it in effect?

Captain Rochefort: I would say yes. Anybody that knew anything about the Japanese or things Japanese would have said when we sent that November 27 letter, "You better run up the red flag because there is trouble coming." Anybody knowing the Japanese would have said that.

Q: That was sent from the State Department.

Captain Rochefort: Yes.

Q: The President and...

Captain Rochefort: That was sent from the President too. All we imposed on the Japanese were three conditions. This would have been extremely difficult for them to have accomplished.

Q: Who were Roosevelt's advisers in the Far East at that time? Do you recall?

Captain Rochefort: No, I don't. Hull, of course, was Secretary of State.*

Q: But it would have been someone in the State Department I presume.

Captain Rochefort: This is the basis for this big discussion that's been going on now for possibly 20 to 25 years or so. The so-called revisionists' activity by the historians, who, not liking FDR, blame him for getting us into the war. Which is true, but we don't know what pressure was brought on him, because at this time we had what was considered a major threat in Europe from Hitler and this takes precedence over everything else. Mr. Roosevelt, you recall, was unable to get us in the war. The Lend-Lease Act only passed by one vote or so.

Q: The draft was just barely passed.

Captain Rochefort: The draft was just barely passed. They still had this feeling left over from World War I

---
*Cordell Hull.

about, you know, we helped you chaps once. It cost us X number of dollars, and we're not about to do it again until you pay your World War I debts and all that sort of thing.

Q: You were telling me what your experience in Japan had been to give you an understanding of the Japanese mind, and I believe you were citing this ultimatum as one of the examples of how being Japanese, they almost had to react.

Captain Rochefort: Yes, I've said before in talking with other people that had the contents of the November 27 message to the Japanese been sent to Admiral Kimmel that I believe sincerely that there were at least two or three people out there who would have recognized this for what it was, and that is an actual ultimatum.[*] The Japanese could not accept this; therefore, the only alternative for the Japanese was to go to war.

Q: It wasn't known generally by the American people either.

Captain Rochefort: No, no. I didn't see this November 27 message until 1944.

---

[*] Admiral Husband E. Kimmel, USN, Commander in Chief Pacific Fleet at the time of the Japanese attack on Pearl Harbor. He maintained afterward that he had not been kept adequately informed by people in Washington.

Rochefort - 72

Q: Has it ever been made public by the historians?

Captain Rochefort: In its entirety, yes. But this information was never furnished to some of the commanders such as General Short and Kimmel.* This information was not made available to them. On the contrary, when General Short received his first so-called war warning, he replied to General Marshall as to what steps he had taken which were completely anti-sabotage measures.** This is one reason they found all the Army planes all bunched up on the strips. Admiral Kimmel did not notify Admiral Stark as to what he was doing but he just assumed that Admiral Stark would expect him to do it, which was to take reasonable precautions but nothing about getting all the ships to sea or doing this or doing that because nothing could be done.*** It would be far preferable to lose the ships in Pearl Harbor where they could be saved later on rather than sending them out to sea, say, 50 miles where if they sink you're never going to get them back. It was far better to have done what he did.

Q: That's an interesting observation.

---
*Lieutenant General Walter C. Short, Commanding General of the Army's Hawaiian Department in December 1941.
**General George C. Marshall, U.S. Army Chief of Staff in 1941.
***Admiral Harold R. Stark, USN, Chief of Naval Operations in 1941.

Rochefort - 73

Captain Rochefort: I'm trying to indicate what the general situation was at that time.

Q: I want to pursue that in some detail too when we get to the 1941 period. I was wondering if you did know any other examples of understanding the Japanese mind that you picked up from living in Tokyo?

Captain Rochefort: None just related strictly to the military.

Q: But I mean just as people or military.

Captain Rochefort: No, except that at that time, of course, the Japanese had this very highly developed clan system. Really what it was was a family system where the senior one was responsible for the rest of the family; the older ones were responsible for the rest of the family. They had this very highly developed. And second, of course, the Emperor was divine and most of the Japanese still believed in that. Then in the military, you had some people in the Navy who traveled somewhat extensively in the Occident or in the West, and they had a fair idea of what went on in the rest of the world and these people were extremely capable and extremely intelligent, including Admiral Yamamoto, who had spent some time in the United States. But at the same time, Yamamoto was a Japanese naval officer and to him doubtless, the Emperor was still divine and whenever orders came from him, this was it. These are the only ones to be carried out.

Q: Who influenced the Emperor?

Captain Rochefort: Well, lots of people at that time thought that the Emperor was more or less a nonentity. He was being used by the military. If this were true, then blame would have to be more on the Army that would be willing, because in the Navy he had some very capable people. But the Army, in distinction from the Navy, very rarely had an opportunity to get out of Japan, and the only thing they knew was really China and Manchuria and possibly Korea. And these people had a very parochial feeling. Not having the opportunity to associate, say, with Germans or British or ourselves, they wouldn't know very much about the rest of the world as some Japanese captain in the Navy. His world was completely wrapped up in marching or firing or training all the day, women and liquor at night, all in Japan, which is all this soldier really knows, he'd be fighting only the Chinese. So he would have not much of a knowledge of the world.

Q: So your feeling was that the Emperor was influenced

more by military-army circles than...

Captain Rochefort: Rather than by Navy. Now when the Navy was brought into this whole thing, maybe you could explain it easier by, say, Yamamoto. Now he dreamed up this Pearl Harbor idea, but at the same time he told the Japanese leaders in the Privy Council, possibly the Emperor himself, and these other types of people--he told that he could make this work, but if the Japanese don't win very quickly, he's not optimistic about the future, which meant that he didn't expect the Japanese to win.

Q: Did he expect Pearl Harbor to be a fatal blow?

Captain Rochefort: No, he was hoping it would be, I guess. He was hoping, but he knew that if this didn't get the United States out of it right away--in other words, if the United States didn't settle this war possibly in a year or a year and a half, that the Japanese could not win. They just couldn't win. This was well known, but this still doesn't affect their feeling about Japan itself. Japan was being forced into this fight by us. This was their feeling, and therefore they had to take this action.

Q: You were only nine years away from Pearl Harbor when you were in Japan, toward the end of your term anyway.

Did you have a feeling of the strength of the military on the Emperor and a warlike atmosphere buildup?

Captain Rochefort: Yes, you could detect this without any particular problem, just in the way they spoke and in their actions also. They were very polite to us and courteous to us, but this was because we were attached to the embassy, and as such we were guests of the Japanese Government. So they were not prone to treating us discourteously. You'd get some of these people, particularly the younger ones, they would tell you very frankly that they still disliked very strenuously the exclusion act of--what was it?--'23 or '24. They still resented this, and they resented being treated as a poor relation. After all, they were a first class world power. They proved this against Russia and against the Chinese. So there was always this feeling-- I'm not speaking now of the general feeling in the United States or in the United States Navy--that sooner or later we are going to have to fight the Japanese. I'm not speaking of this. I'm speaking of the more definite thing. Unless one of the two gives a little ground, we are going to go to war. This was generally expected.

Q: The Navy war games for years had been to fight Japan anyway.

Captain Rochefort: They had always been against Orange, they had always been.* We had always considered Orange as the logical enemy. But our trouble was that when we'd get...

Q: We didn't do anything to abate that, it would appear, also.

Captain Rochefort: No, we did not. We made no effort.

Q: You started to say, it would appear...

Captain Rochefort: It would appear that if the two of us sat down and reasoned the problem out, but further complicating these things, of course, at this time in '41, was the situation in Europe. And this was the overriding thing at that time. I would not criticize a person in the slightest because...

Q: Criticize who?

Captain Rochefort: I would not criticize the President, because he had information available to him which we didn't have and after all, he makes the decisions. I would not

---

*In war games conducted by the U.S. Navy between the World Wars, Japan was given the code name Orange and considered the potential enemy.

criticize his decision if it meant getting us into war, because I just didn't know what was going on on the other side of the world.

Q: Do you know what the Navy's developments or activities in cryptography were during the period that you were in Japan?

Captain Rochefort: Yes, just from my friends is all. Of course, when I'd be attached to this staff or that staff, sometimes there was information made available to us.

Q: But I meant particularly when you were in Japan, did you relate the Japanese language knowledge to the fact that you were going to then go back into cryptography?

Captain Rochefort: Oh no, I had no intention of going back to it.

Q: You didn't?

Captain Rochefort: No, not at that time.

Q: Why did you think you were being sent to learn the Japanese language?

Captain Rochefort: For possible use in cryptanalysis. But I was not about to ask for this sort of duty.

Q: You knew it was related to it, but you were not going to press the issue.

Captain Rochefort: I wasn't going to press the issue, no.

Q: During those years, were you kept aware of what the advances were or the activities were in the Navy's cryptographic...

Captain Rochefort: Yes, I was, generally from the people who were involved. Possibly Safford and people like that. Then every time I went through Washington, of course, I would go down to the Navy Department and talk to these people.

Q: Were they making any great strides in the field or not?

Captain Rochefort: I would say not. We had, I recall, our good periods and our bad periods. Sometimes we would be successful, sometimes we wouldn't be successful. We would go for periods of time, say, when they put a new cipher into effect, that we'd be unable to read the stuff, and this would be considered a black time and sooner or later we would be successful. But it became increasingly difficult. I noticed that all during the Thirties. It became increasingly difficult, so the successes were not too many.

Q: Did you have any time for extracurricular activities when you were in Japan? Did you enjoy the personal side of it at all?

Captain Rochefort: Oh yes, that was a very, very pleasant interlude. Both with the official side of it, that is, going to parties and one thing and another--i.e. the Chrysanthemum party of the Emperor's and Cherry Blossom Time, and we would, of course, go to the Palace on New Year's, naturally; that's standard procedure over there. And we took many trips around.

Q: Did you make many friends among the Japanese?

Captain Rochefort: Yes, I think we did. We made quite a few friends. But as time rolled on, we didn't communicate with these people. I think our maid kept up communication for about a year about her husband and so on and so forth but not the regular official communications. Occasionally

Rochefort - 81

we might see somebody around Washington that we had seen in Tokyo, just like passing friends.

Q: Well, I imagine you hated to leave that duty, and what did you ask for next, or did they ask you what you wanted?

Captain Rochefort: No, when I left Japan, of course, I had to go back to Washington for temporary duty, and I asked a friend of mine back there who had been one of the naval attachés in Tokyo, Captain Ogan, and I respected him very highly.[*] I asked him, where should I go next? He told me to get on a battleship and the bigger the better, the newest one. So I was ordered to the Maryland for ship duty. I was scheduled to become a turret officer, which is with the gunnery department. And before I could take over, I received a letter from a Captain Glassford,[**] who was assistant director of naval communications in '25-'27, and he asked me to serve as his assistant on the Battle Force staff. Admiral Standley was being ordered as Commander Battle Force and he had, of course, obviously asked for Captain Glassford to be his operations officer.[***] Captain Glassford asked me to be his assistant, possibly from our

---
[*] Captain Joseph V. Ogan, USN, who was then serving in the Office of Naval Intelligence in Washington.
[**] Captain William A. Glassford, Jr., USN, later a flag officer during World War II.
[***] Admiral William H. Standley, USN, became Chief of Naval Operations in July 1933 after a few weeks as Commander Battle Force.

days in the Office of Naval Communications. I accepted this. In the meantime, very rapidly, Admiral Standley was ordered to Washington to become Chief of Naval Operations and Admiral Reeves who had been ordered as Commander Battleships then moved up to become Commander Battle Force.[*] But he kept the same staff that Admiral Standley had selected.

Q: Are you leaving out the period that you served in ONI?

Captain Rochefort: That was just a temporary duty there about two or three months.

Q: I have from October '32 to March '33, which would be about five months.

Captain Rochefort: Well, most of that five months was engaged in travel. At that time, we just didn't send people by air. In the first place, there wasn't any air, and the second thing was cost. So in going from the East Coast to the West Coast, I traveled on a destroyer down to Panama and up as far as San Pedro.

Q: So actually there was no duty at ONI.

Captain Rochefort: No duty at ONI. No, there was no duty

---

[*] Admiral Joseph M. Reeves, USN.

involved. It was just all mostly travel. I think also there was a fleet problem in the midst of that in which I was ordered for temporary duty to some staff in connection with this cryptographic stuff. I think there was a fleet problem for a couple of months or so. But we didn't get settled down until after Admiral Standley left and Admiral Reeves had become Commander Battle Force. And at that point I was made the assistant operations officer for Captain Glassford and additional duty as fleet intelligence officer. I stayed there for three years.

Q: That was from the time that you went on the Maryland through the Battle Force and to the staff of Commander in Chief, U.S. Fleet. You were assistant operations officer.

Captain Rochefort: Assistant fleet operations officer and fleet intelligence officer and a general handyman. As I said before, a utility man and a confidant of Admiral Reeves.

Q: You had said earlier that perhaps being coddled or made a protégé of some person might have not been good for your career, and was this one of the situations of which you referred?

Captain Rochefort: Yes, because Admiral Reeves was quite

a person, and he did a lot of rather unorthodox things. He would try to bring the fleet to a higher peak of efficiency, and doing this he undoubtedly stepped on some people's toes and then they would, with some reasonableness, they would ascribe his actions to some of these younger people that Admiral Reeves had surrounded himself with, and I had reason to believe that this affected some actions later on.

Q: Can you give me a for instance?

Captain Rochefort: Not particularly. I remember when I was transferred from the staff to shore duty in San Pedro, as a branch of the district intelligence office which was in San Diego. Actually, I was a sort of liaison officer for commander in chief. When I reported for duty in San Diego, there was a memorandum there stating that when I reported to duty I was to report to the admiral in person. I did so, and he proceeded to quiz me pretty thoroughly on why the commander in chief did this, that, and the other thing. So I could detect the feeling right there. There were quite a few instances of this nature, but it doesn't make any difference. I just had that feeling that I was probably being treated a little easier than maybe I should have been treated as a lieutenant.

Rochefort - 85

Q: Did you enjoy your duties during these three years?

Captain Rochefort: Oh yes, this was fantastic, because again I was serving at the very top level in the fleet. It was a far cry from there down to, say, commanding a destroyer or something like this. Oh yes, that was remarkable duty, and I enjoyed it.

Q: What was the ship's operations then?

Captain Rochefort: The staff was responsible for the operations of the fleet.

Q: But where were they operating? Just off the West Coast?

Captain Rochefort: Oh no, they would be all over as United States Fleet. This also took care of the Atlantic Fleet. We were the senior people afloat in the Navy.

Q: Where did you go? I wanted you to describe where you went and where the fleet went and...

Captain Rochefort: We'd have fleet problems every year, and the drawing up of this fleet problem and one thing and another and development of the various annexes such as who was going to anchor where and the order of ships and the planned exercises--all of this was done by the Commander in Chief United States Fleet. He prepared the operations plans for movements from the West Coast to the East Coast and, of course, its return. This is what I'm referring to as operations. We assigned periods of time for people to conduct gunnery operations. We did all of this. We prepared anchorage charts for the fleet. In many cases, we assigned the anchorages to the various flagships. This is what I'm talking about in the fleet as operations. At the same time we were attempting, in the admiral's words, to bring the fleet "up to snuff." This is what I am referring to.

Q: In what regard did he think it was not up to snuff?

Captain Rochefort: Well, you've heard the expression, "a new broom sweeps clean." This is it. Any commander of a ship or a group of ships or a fleet or anything else, when he takes over command, obviously he is going to improve this thing. So he must think very much about how it operated last year. Then his job is to improve both the morale and training and efficiency and the skill and one thing and another of the units of the fleet. Then when he finishes his tour of duty and his relief comes aboard, all these things are repeated and this is the way it worked. We had a couple of interesting fleet problems during this

Rochefort - 87

period of time. We moved the fleet from the West Coast to the East Coast and spent the summer on the East Coast which was generally political. It's known as showing the flag.

Q: Was Congress considering cutting appropriations or something?

Captain Rochefort: No, to show the residents on the East Coast what they're paying for. Showing the flag or anything of this nature--what you want to call it--and then when the fleet came back in the fall to the West Coast for all of our training--gunnery training, engineering training. We made a cruise to Hawaii in which we took the fleet to Hawaii and engaged in operations out there. That lasted until Admiral Reeves went to shore duty and actually to retirement and then, of course, it came time for me to go to shore duty. I went to shore duty, and this job was closely connected with the fleet as the fleet liaison.

Q: I was wondering. It's indicated as Headquarters Eleventh Naval District.

Captain Rochefort: Well, technically my immediate superior was the district intelligence officer in San Diego. He was told not to bother me, and I was just more or less independent. I was actually on shore duty, but I was really working for commander in chief.

Q: Communications intelligence?

Captain Rochefort: Liaison officer and working with the City of Los Angeles and the County of Los Angeles and that sort of thing. That was rather interesting too.

Q: What was the liaison? When the ships were going to visit a port, to work out the plans?

Captain Rochefort: No. As an example or maybe a very poor example, commander in chief might be invited to a function in Los Angeles, and he would want to know what this was all about. Who was this individual sponsoring this function and what was his relationship to the Navy and what was expected of him in return, so that he wouldn't embarrass himself and embarrass the Navy by being present at something where he shouldn't have been. And I was expected to inform him of the host's position in Los Angeles in any relation whatever to the Navy. That was my function then.

Q: Who was the commander in chief then?

Captain Rochefort: Admiral Hepburn and Admiral Bloch, I believe.*

Q: You did that roughly for two years, just a regular two-year duty.

Captain Rochefort: Yes.

Q: And then you followed the regular schedule and went back to sea.

Captain Rochefort: As navigator of a heavy cruiser.

Q: And you enjoyed that again, too?

Captain Rochefort: Yes. Well, somebody told me one time the two best jobs in the Navy were navigator of a ship or in command of a ship. Of course, I couldn't command anything at that time but a minesweeper, maybe, so the navigator was my best job. Navigator of a heavy cruiser was particularly desirable in that they were somewhat similar to destroyers, a lot of speed and a lot of power, and so they were very comfortable. They were almost as comfortable at sea as a battleship. This was a lot of fun. Also,

---
*Admiral Arthur J. Hepburn, USN; Admiral Claude C. Bloch, USN.

you were still in the Grand Fleet then, traveling with the high class, not being around the dregs or the backwaters. I thoroughly enjoyed that. It was very enjoyable duty.

Q: You were away from all of the actual intelligence and cryptographic work for a long time and from the language. How did you maintain your proficiency during these years?

Captain Rochefort: I just kept up with the language and all, by studying and reading books and by translating books or documents.

Q: Officially or just for your own?

Captain Rochefort: On my own. On several occasions I would be asked to translate something which I would be very glad to do. I kept up pretty well while still performing these other duties. There was no particular problem then.

Q: But you still did it. No one asked you to or required you to. You did it on your own.

Captain Rochefort: No, no one. Well, of course, the jobs themselves too--now when I was at San Pedro as the liaison man with commander in chief then at that time, of course, we were interested in Japanese activities on the West Coast and also Russia. In my assigned duty, which was that of assistant district intelligence officer for this particular area around southern California, I would have some dealings with the Japanese to the extent of being asked occasionally the itinerary or location of some Japanese individual. I'd be asked to do this. This involved close relationship with the Japanese community up in Los Angeles.

Q: Did you have a chance then to use your language?

Captain Rochefort: Then I used my language, and I had the opportunity.

Q: Would you have any particular anecdotes of interest during your tour on the New Orleans?

Captain Rochefort: No. It was extremely pleasant.

Q: You actually had four years after you left the headquarters, didn't you? No, one year on the New Orleans and then two years on the scouting force.

Captain Rochefort: I was two years on the New Orleans, wasn't I? '37 to '39?

Q: This says '38 to '39 on the New Orleans.

Rochefort - 92

Captain Rochefort: It should read '37 to '39. I think it was '37. I think I spent a little over two years on there. Because I had two captains. I had Captain Beauregard and Captain Purnell.*

Q: Why do I know that name Purnell? Beauregard.

Captain Rochefort: Of the New Orleans Beauregards. Augustine Toutant Beauregard was his name.

Q: Well, this indicates, incorrectly then, that you were two years, from '36--almost exactly two years, June '36 to June '38--in the Headquarters Eleventh Naval District and then June '38 to September '39 on the New Orleans which would have been a year and three months, and then '39 to '41 on Staff Commander Scouting Force, Pacific Fleet, on the Indianapolis.

Captain Rochefort: Yes. Commander Scouting Force is the same of course as Commander Hawaiian Detachment. I would have said--maybe you're right. If you got these figures from the Bureau of Personnel, then they should be more correct than mine.

Q: Not necessarily. Many of them are not accurate.

---
*Captain William R. Purnell, USN.

Rochefort - 93

Captain Rochefort: Well, in any event, I would have said I spent about two years on the New Orleans. It doesn't make any difference, one way or the other.

Q: You went from one sea duty then to another sea duty. From the New Orleans to the...

Captain Rochefort: Staff of the Commander Scouting Force which was [Vice] Admiral Adolphus Andrews, yes. That would be in the fall of '39. I'm reasonably sure of that date also.

Q: That does agree. You were telling me about it being-- would you mind repeating for me the makeup of this Hawaiian Detachment.

Captain Rochefort: I think the Hawaiian Detachment was probably the first example of a task force which had been organized for a specific purpose. It was an operational command--the Hawaiian Detachment. But the administrative command was Scouting Force. The operational command would have been something less than Scouting Force, but we called it the Hawaiian Detachment. Its purpose, being ordered to Pearl Harbor, its major purpose, the real reason was that we would have here a task force which would be capable of air attacks--to a lesser extent, ship attacks, gun attacks, to be based 2,000 miles closer to Tokyo than the rest of the fleet was and could act as a very strong, very offensive arm of the fleet--more for offensive purposes than anything else.

Q: What was the makeup of this detachment?

Captain Rochefort: Two carriers and all the heavy cruisers, 16, or actually it was about 12, because you always had one heavy cruiser in the Asiatic Fleet and a couple of cruisers in overhaul. But these were the heavy cruisers with 8-inch shells. One squadron of destroyers and the necessary repair ships and tankers; we went out to Pearl in the fall of '39 and remained out there. Then gradually, of course, on the outbreak of war they broke up this organization and assigned them to various other commands.

Q: What was the atmosphere or the tension, if any, in the fleet during those days?

Captain Rochefort: There was a little bit of tension among some of the more senior officers but certainly not among the crew. But there was a feeling--we all knew that the war was coming. It was a question of getting ready for it, if and when the war came. And then there was no question as to who was to win this war. Incidentally, there were no demonstrations or anything else. We still had men with strong feelings and men of loyalty.

Q: Of course, the Hawaiian Detachment had just been sent out in anticipation pretty much of what did happen.

Captain Rochefort: For that purpose, yes. Of course, if you will relate all of '39, this was the time when World War II started in Europe--August of '39. So, of course, it was directly related to that.

Q: When did the battleships go out?

Captain Rochefort: The rest of the Grand Fleet came out the following spring, that would be in the spring of '40. They came out then at that time.

Q: And then became based in Pearl Harbor instead of the West Coast.

Captain Rochefort: Yes. What it amounted to then, you have the whole Battle Force and Scouting Force on station at Pearl Harbor. You've got both the major forces in the United States Fleet out there. I believe also that some additional submarines were brought out from the West Coast so we got all the submarines out there too, the major submarines.

Rochefort - 96

Q: So, in any case, do you have any further anecdotes about this Scouting Force or the Indianapolis or any of those days that you were at sea before May '41?

Captain Rochefort: When we went out to Pearl, we found to our horror that Pearl Harbor and the Navy Yard would practically close up shop on Wednesday afternoon and on Friday afternoon. There was no activity there on Saturday at all. Well, we immediately speeded these people up. Then, when the Grand Fleet came out the next spring, then they speeded us up. We were apparently in the meantime starting to slow down with the Hawaiian atmosphere.

I would say at that particular moment, say when the big ships came out to Pearl Harbor, the fleet was very well organized and very well prepared. You see what happened was, unfortunately, you've got a war in Europe here going on and gradually this became very serious--the war in Europe--so that they required practically all the materiel that we needed in Pearl, which instead of that, it was going to Europe.

Q: And 50 of our destroyers, as I recall.

Captain Rochefort: Well, we didn't need that pile of junk anyway, but we could have used the airplanes, but they were all going to England, and most of our materiel was going to England. And all we were supposed to do apparently was to keep the flag flying and not cause any trouble. This resulted in a major shortage then in 1941, because the main effort at that time was in training. Well, it had to be. We were prepared at this stage of the game to keep England going and to keep France going, not to mention Russia, which was slight, but you had to keep these people going too. So the net effect was that we were getting very little out in the Pacific.

Q: What caused your transfer at this particular time? Was it the end of a tour and you were due to go back to shore duty in May '41?

Captain Rochefort: No, May '41--they had made, within the communications intelligence organization, a major policy decision--I say "they"--this would be primarily, Safford. At that time, the communication intelligence organization was operated primarily from Washington, and then it had what you might call a little outpost or station, one at Pearl Harbor and one in the Philippines called Cavite or Cast. It was a very small organization, and a major effort was made down in Washington. Honolulu, or Hypo as it was called, was not particularly active. Dyer was in charge there. No, Birtley, I guess it was, was in charge.*

---

*Lieutenant Commander Thomas B. Birtley, Jr., USN.

But nothing much was being accomplished and we were not reading very much stuff at that time either. So they decided to build up Hypo if necessary at the expense of the home station in Washington and transfer many of the activities they were then doing in Washington to Station Hypo. They found out where I was, and I was due for shore duty anyway. So they had me ordered to take over command of Hypo station. That would be about in May or June of '41. But it was the result of a policy decision to upgrade Hypo and give them additional responsibility. Most of this was done in personal letters between Safford and myself.

Q: Oh, I see. So you knew where you were going, and why.

Captain Rochefort: Yes, I had a pretty good idea of where I was going to go and I was due for shore duty, so it didn't come as any surprise. Safford and I had been in communication off and on for the last 10 or 12 years.

Q: He was back in Washington now?

Captain Rochefort: He was back there permanently, because he transferred over to engineering duty only. In other words, he was all through with going to sea and he became what we called an EDO so that he could stay there in that job.

Q: In intelligence?

Captain Rochefort: No, he was still working for communications in charge of the whole communications/intelligence organization. But operating under communications. This is one of those problem areas I was talking to you about in the very beginning. So he, prior to the outbreak of war, he was in charge of Op-20-G* and at the same time, he had more or less loosely under his control, Station Hypo, which was me, and the small station on Cavite which was being run by a fellow named Fabian--you know, more or less loosely.** Unfortunately, most of this was done on a personal basis, that is by means of letters and notes and that sort of thing. As long as Safford was in Washington, I just about knew what to expect from him, and he knew what he could expect from me. It worked very nicely on a personal basis. It was only then when other people became involved in it as a part of the expansion that we began to have trouble.

Q: What kind of trouble?

Captain Rochefort: Mostly people seeking glory. You'd get people who would want to be in this organization for

---

*Op-20-G--the communications intelligence section on the OpNav staff.
**Lieutenant Rudolph J. Fabian, USN

their own personal purposes, not for what they could offer. One of these people would be a chap named Jack Redman who saw a chance here to what Rudyard Kipling used to say--the promotion and pay.* He took this road, with the net effect that Safford was sort of eased out of the job that he had, and he was stuck over in a corner somewhere, I know we didn't utilize his talents. That was one of the things.

The second thing was to have somebody on Hypo that would be a creature of his, and this obviously was not going to be Rochefort. But that was one of the end results. Not a reorganization but just bringing in people.

Q: Was it in an effort to give it more stature? That is, larger personnel, bigger?

Captain Rochefort: That was a personal gain for some people, you see, because, if handled properly, you can make a pretty big thing out of this.

Q: I would think so.

Captain Rochefort: ...In the way of personal glory, you can make a pretty big thing out of it. But, in any event, I was ordered there in May, possibly June of '41 from my

---
*Commander John R. Redman, USN

duty on the Scouting Force staff. And I remained there until October of '42.

Q: Ladislas Farago again, to quote him, says, "Commander Rochefort, senior member of the secret fraternity and the Navy's foremost cryptologist, was at sea in the Indianapolis, flagship of the Scouting Force, Pacific Fleet--in an effort to crack the new code in Washington, Safford was reassembling the team that had started American cryptography off on the road to purple with its pioneering recovery of the red machine and Rochefort was drawn into it again in May 1941. His group and he--he--was called the dean of the Navy cryptanalysts."

Captain Rochefort: No, Safford would be the senior one. Because Safford gradually got away from the dog work of cryptanalysis--he got away from this and this was left up to some other people, younger people. Safford gradually gave more and more attention to the security of our own system. He became more and more involved in secrecy--designing new machinery and this, that, and the other thing--rather than strictly cryptanalysis. He became quite intrigued with these new systems that were being developed.

Q: You, then, were in fact the dean of the Navy's cryptanalysts.

Captain Rochefort: Well, in a sense, yes. But during this period of time--say during the Thirties, for example--I was involved primarily in ship duty and staff duty. And I doubt that I would have exerted any influence whatever in this area of cryptanalysis, because I was involved in ship duty, which was my first choice.

Q: Is there a need to keep up with cryptanalysis?

Captain Rochefort: Oh, yes.

Q: That's why I was wondering how you could have gone this nine years and then come back in to be the officer in charge of this terribly important unit.

Captain Rochefort: Well, during this period of time--actually I'd say about a 12-year period of time--you don't get any great developments in this period of time. You measure the advances either during a war or during a period of 30 or 50 or 75 years. But you don't measure this overnight. So when I got involved again, you see, it was essentially about the same--the same problems, the same difficulties and everything--it had, say, 15 years before. But the reason, I think, that Hypo was successful--I'm trying now to be--not modest and not immodest--but it was because part of my arrangement with Safford was that I'll undertake this job, but I'll get my pick of the personnel. Now, if you want to go ahead and build yourself another outfit in Washington, this is fine and dandy. But I'll take this job providing I can keep Dyer and I can get first shot at anybody else whom I need and I get all the language officers. These were the conditions. Safford said, "You can have anything you want." So the organization in Pearl beginning in the fall of 1941 and extending until the time I left there--these people were the pick of the crop.

Q: Who did you have besides Dyer?

Captain Rochefort: I had Dyer, and a fellow named "Ham" Wright--these would be cryptanalysts and just about as good as they come.[*] Then I had possibly the two best language officers--I like to think, besides me--this would be Joe Finnegan and a Marine, a fellow named Lasswell.[**] We had very excellent officers, too, for radio intelligence; it was very difficult to keep these people there, just wallowing around in the area of intelligence for about seven or eight years.

Q: What was his name?

---

[*] Lieutenant Wesley A. Wright, USN.
[**] Lieutenant Joseph Finnegan, USN; Captain Alva B. Lasswell, USMC.

Captain Rochefort: That would be Tom Huckins and Jack Williams.* These people were very difficult to beat for what we called radio intelligence. Radio intelligence does not involve the content of the message, just in the heading. What can you get out of the heading itself? Who originated the message and who is on the receiving end of this message? What relationship are they? And from this you can associate. For example, you get one fellow who is talking say to about 15 or 20 or 30 apparently ship commanders and all of these ship commanders have been identified as submariners, isn't it rather obvious then that the man is sending a message to a group of submariners about submarine operations?

Q: That was especially then within your office--radio intelligence?

Captain Rochefort: Yes, this was a part of communications intelligence, because you cannot expect to be forever reading these messages. You've got to be able to put yourself in a position where you expect a lot of information just from the messages themselves without being able to read them. This generally is known as radio intelligence, it's a part of it. Like direction finding was the same thing, where a fellow sends a message and by means of radio direction finders you ascertain his geographical position. Then this

---

*Lieutenant Commander Thomas A. Huckins, USN; Lieutenant John A. Williams, USN.

tells you sometimes who he is. That's called direction finding, DF. That's a part of radio intelligence.

We developed--I would say with all modesty that this was the best communications intelligence organization that this world has ever seen. But it was due simply to the fact that the people whom we had there were the tops in their particular fields and all together like a team. They had been in this business anywhere from five to ten or twelve years, and I had been involved in this thing since 1925 and I fancied myself as a translator and gradually became more and more involved in the translation aspects of it. This is the crux of the whole thing. You can assign values and all that sort of thing, but unless you do a good job of translating then the whole value is lost.

Q: Can you give me a for instance of that?

Captain Rochefort: Yes. You're reading a message and one translator might say this reads as follows, that I might under certain circumstances do so and so. He might translate it this way. If I looked at this thing, I'd say no, this is not right. Under certain circumstances I <u>will</u> do this thing. It's a big difference, you know.

Q: Yes, very much.

Captain Rochefort: It was that sort of thing.

Q: Was that a nuance in the language or an actual translation?

Captain Rochefort: Well, you can make what you call a rough translation of French to English or English to French or German or anything else. You might give a rough translation or you might give a very careful translation. So much can depend on whether it is going to be "will," "shall," or something like this, you see. I wanted to look these translations over. This was the major task in the whole thing. One of the things that's confusing a lot of people, and it still does, I think, was the Battle of Leyte, where Kurita* after getting into the Leyte Gulf, was in an enviable position with Halsey charging out after the Japanese somewhere, in the next five minutes or so, he (Kurita) could completely disrupt the whole Leyte operation.** It might inflict extremely serious damage to us. He, for some unexplainable reason, reversed his course and left the area, sparing our transports and those flattops we had down there and all those people. If he had just stayed another five minutes, he could have made a shambles out of Leyte Gulf. Why did he retreat? This has been the occasion for a couple of

---
*Vice Admiral Takeo Kurita, IJN, Commander of the First Striking Force at Leyte Gulf.
**Admiral William F. Halsey, Jr., USN, Commander Third Fleet.

million words, I suppose. In his original battle report that he sent back to Tokyo--Admiral Kurita sent back to Tokyo--in his original battle report, which I translated, at one time he used an expression which is very seldom used and what it actually means is "for the time being"--this is the actual meaning of the partial message that he sent--that he had reversed course and headed back up toward San Bernardino Strait. He gave as his reason to the Navy Department, "for the time being I have reversed my course"--this is the literal translation--but it could be read, "I am reversing course, period." He's not about to say retreat because you can't retreat. The Japanese never retreat. They might reverse, but they don't retreat. Or like the Marines up there in Korea coming off the reservoir, going off the hill, they said they were advancing to the rear. That was the expression they used when they were getting the hell out of there as fast as they could--but they never retreat. They just advanced to the rear. This expression was somewhat similar to that. It was an expression you could only get if you were quite familiar with the Japanese language. You've got to sort of read between the lines. And this was exactly what he meant, that he was retreating. He says he's reversing course for the time being. Now this had been variously translated as in order to reorganize, in order to regroup, in order to do something else. This is the reason that translation is extremely important.

Q: Well, what did the effect of this have? You say if he had stayed another five minutes.

Captain Rochefort: If he had kept on going, he would have had an excellent chance of destroying a large number of our vessels--people involved in the landing, and he should certainly have no problem whatever with the little Kaiser aircraft carriers--they're flattops.* He could have destroyed about a dozen of those. And he could have disrupted the whole operation.

Q: Well, what did the translation have to do with his maneuver?

Captain Rochefort: The translation explained--he makes a battle report to the Navy Department, the Japanese Navy Department, after this is over and he gives as his reason why he left this area, why he in other words reversed course and got out of the area--he gave as his reason for this, "for the time being." He never expanded on it beyond that. But the crux of the translation lay in what did he mean when he said he reversed course and then these couple of groups--what did he mean? What was he talking about?

---

*Kaiser escort carriers were small carriers intended primarily for antisubmarine escort duty and for transporting planes between theaters; they were not intended for the sort of fleet engagement they encountered at Leyte.

Many people say tht he lost his nerve. Well, this was a very stupid thing to say. In the first place, this guy had been involved in receiving attacks for the previous 48 hours--first, by submarines; next, by Halsey's carriers--he had been attacked for 11 consecutive hours in approaching the San Bernardino Strait by Halsey's carriers. And this was really his third day down there that this guy was under extreme pressure, so he's not chicken. But he could be mentally exhausted or physically exhausted, which is probably what happened. He was not thinking straight. But in any event I started off this thing by giving an example of what value a translation has.

Q: But that did not affect our battle at all.

Captain Rochefort: Oh, no, no. The only difference being that he didn't destroy Admiral Kinkaid's group; that ws the big difference. By his actions, Admiral Kinkaid was safe.*

Q: Did the American fleet--they were not aware of his message, were they? When he said I am...

Captain Rochefort: Oh, no. No, this was written after the battle was all over.

---

*Vice Admiral Thomas C. Kinkaid, USN, Commander Seventh Fleet.

Rochefort - 110

Q: You were just giving it as a for instance of the nuance between the actual translation.

Captain Rochefort: Yes, between this Japanese. An ordinary translator might have just said that I'm reversing course, I am retreating, I am changing direction, or something of this nature. This is not what he said. He was apparently a little bit mentally confused himself, I'm referring to Kurita now, who was the commander of the Japanese Fleet, the Kido Butai and I'm forgetting the thing myself, you know. But during the period out here in Hypo, which is what we were talking about, before the war we had what I choose to believe the best organization this world has ever seen. There was a lot of luck attached to this. Also there was the fact that we had all worked together at some time or another and we were all reasonably competent-- Dyer and Wright and Jack Williams, the rest of them were all reasonably competent and they were all determined to build an organization which would save American lives.

Q: Why wasn't this organization able to foresee the Pearl Harbor action?

Captain Rochefort: I personally felt very responsible for that. Nobody has ever blamed us for lack of effort or failure to come up with the right answer. Nobody has ever done this. They have been very kind. But I felt very responsible for this for a long time and I still do. I still feel that we failed in our job. As for excuses, I can offer a lot of excuses. We had only been there for five or six months.

Q: In what way did you mean you failed? Was there traffic that you didn't decode or...

Captain Rochefort: No. I have often said that an intelligence officer has one task, one job, one mission. This is to tell his commander, his superior, today, what the Japanese are going to do tomorrow. This is his job. If he doesn't do this, then he's failed. This is his number one job and only job, and as I've often said there isn't any sense at all in telling General MacArthur, for instance, in late June or July that North Korea has invaded South Korea. He knows this. He can read newspapers. But you've got to tell General MacArthur before June 25, 1950, for this to have any effect, which is where intelligence failed MacArthur during the Korean War and also failed the Navy.[*]

On December the 7th, we did not inform Admiral Kimmel prior to December 7th that the Japanese were going to make an attack.

---

[*] General of the Army Douglas MacArthur, Supreme Commander of United Nations forces in the Korean War.

Rochefort - 112

Q: Did you know they were?

Captain Rochefort: No, therefore we failed.

Q: Well, then the question is why didn't you know?

Captain Rochefort: Well, as I say, I can offer a lot of excuses which would all be alibis. One, we did not have more than about five months to get ourselves reorganized. Secondly, all the material that we asked for was being withheld, because it was being sent to Europe.

Q: What do you mean by material?

Captain Rochefort: Radio equipment. Come December 7th, we're still running the intercept things from the intercept station which was six or eight miles away and running that down by jeep. We should have had numerous teletypes. We could have saved ourselves an hour each time, you see. Instead of that, we still had to run them down in jeeps or bicycles or motorcycles, which was ridiculous. We had a very lousy wire system--I mean by wire system, telephones and all that sort of thing. This was just lousy. It's like having a million-dollar organization with a ten-cent-store communication system.
    We lost communications with our direction finders

right off the bat on December the 7th. This was a major standby thing. We should have been in instant communication with our direction finders so we could communicate with them back and forth. Well, what with the Army yanking out all the wires and every conduit they could get their hands on, there was just general confusion all over. The only way in which we could communicate with our big station, a thing called the CXK out in Lualualei, up near the ammunition dump, was by sending a jeep out there. This would take a couple of hours to get out there and back.

Q: I don't see how you operated at all.

Captain Rochefort: Well, we could operate in peacetime but not during wartime.

Q: Were there messages, do you think, if you had interpreted them that would have told you about Pearl Harbor?

Captain Rochefort: At this particular moment, up to and including December 7th, we were not reading the Japanese system, because the cryptanalysts had failed. We were not reading. They had changed a major part of the system on December 1, and we were just in the black. We were not translating anything from their language. But this doesn't alter the facts, you see. According to my definition of the duties and responsibilities of an intelligence officer, we should have kept Admiral Kimmel informed as to what the Japanese were up to. We did not do this. Therefore, we failed.

Q: I understand your words. But on the other hand, you have to have material. If there were no messages. There were messages.

Captain Rochefort: There were messages, but we couldn't read them.

Q: But you couldn't read them. Had they been working on it in Washington?

Captain Rochefort: Washington and Cavite had been working on it, yes.

Q: But they had not been able to interpret it. Was this what Farago means when he said that efforts were being made in Washington to crack the new code by Safford?

Captain Rochefort: Yes, you see, originally--without getting into too much of the details of it, some of it is still classified I would imagine--we were assigned responsibility when I took over over there for one system which was not

Rochefort - 115

the system that Washington was working on. Washington and Cavite were working on what the Navy called ***************
This was the system.

Q: **?

Captain Rochefort: Well, no, I don't think we ever called it that. I don't think we ever called it a name at all. I don't believe so. **

Q: Different codes that they had that you had broken.

Captain Rochefort: Yes. But ****** we were having no luck. The expression that we use on the thing, I believe, you read it or you don't read it. We were not reading this *****, which is what the Japanese fleet was using. We weren't able to read that up to December 7th. We could extract information from it in connection with radio intelligence or direction finding. We could do this or we could make guesses, which we called estimates about what the message contained. But this would be a pure guess. We were not reading it. By reading, I mean we were just not making English out of it and then passing it on.

Q: Were you passing on what you could guess?

Captain Rochefort: Oh yes, but not the major system. We were passing on a lot of junk which turned out later on to be public works information like the sewers and roads and airports and that sort of thing. We were able to do some of the small stuff and minor stuff but not the big stuff, as of December 7th.

Q: Did you recognize by the size or volume or mass of material that there was something important?

Captain Rochefort: Oh, certainly. We knew that. But they apparently didn't believe it because the cryptanalysts had not been able to solve it.

Q: Were you upset about it?

Captain Rochefort: Sure. Actually up to December 7th, this was not our job. This was not one of the tasks that had been assigned to us. So anything we did on this, we did it on our own.

Q: Oh, they were doing it in Washington.

Captain Rochefort: They were doing it in Washington and Cavite, yes. We were not doing it.

Rochefort - 117

Q: You were assigned another...

Captain Rochefort: We were assigned another major task.

Q: A major code to break, another system?

Captain Rochefort: We were assigned another system or systems to read, and this had been our main assignment from June until December. Then on December 10th or thereabouts, then we scrapped this other thing we were working on--we forgot this whole business and turned to on the one that was in use in which 50 or 75% of the traffic was being sent. We concentrated on that, and that is the thing that gave us our successes later on. But we always kept reading this thing.

Q: You say you had only been there five months. That seems like a long time to me. But this is not long...

Captain Rochefort: Oh, in cryptographic work, heavens, you can fiddle with something for a number of years.

Q: You spoke of Miss Aggie working on something for a year as though...

Captain Rochefort: Prior to solution.

Q: Yes, prior to solution. Then five months would not be any time at all in history.

Captain Rochefort: Oh no, no. You see, this is one of the troubles. If you solve the system, this solution is only good until the enemy changes. And this could just be overnight.

Q: Yes. You might solve it today and they change it tomorrow or yesterday.

Captain Rochefort: I can recall--oh, later on, in August, before we made our landings in Guadalcanal--by this time, they had been ********* I guess. They were using ***** which is the one they used beginning in June 1, 1942. And we were well into reading this thing. We were having no problems at all. We had had a couple of lucky breaks. In August we were doing quite well and then some eager Marine out on Guadalcanal dug up one or more of those Japanese codes that the Japanese had buried prior to going off, and they were very proud of themselves. They sent that thing up to me, and all I could do was curse the whole Marine Corps. You see, that's the last thing we wanted. We didn't want to see this lousy book. We were reading stuff. But when the Japanese realized it was lost, then they made a big change.

Rochefort - 119

Q: Oh, of course.

Captain Rochefort: And then you've got to start all over again.

Q: Of course, they know it's compromised.

Captain Rochefort: They know it's compromised and they start all over again. All we did was curse this well-meaning Marine. Anyway, getting back to this other thing, the decision was made to forget this one system that had been assigned us and handle ****** in conjunction with Washington and Cavite--attack this one system exclusively. And we started to work on that, and Washington and Cavite were to assist us. We were to take the lead on it and they were to assist us. So I'd say maybe about February we really got into this business and got ourselves organized. I picked up another 50 or 75 men, and I had an understanding with the chief personnel officer as the drafts were coming into Pearl from the West Coast, they'd line all these guys up and they'd have their service record with them and we would pick out the people we wanted.

Q: You got the first choice.

Captain Rochefort: First choice of all personnel, including

the registrar of the University of California at Berkeley. He was one of them.

Q: Really. What was his name?

Captain Rochefort: I've forgotten now. But being registrar he was probably a personal friend of Admiral Nimitz. But anyway he got working for me. We built up our force that way by glancing at the service records. Of course, we previously got the whole band from the California, I think. The California or the Arizona.

Q: One of the ships that was destroyed?

Captain Rochefort: Yes. We had the band more or less intact.

Q: They had the what?

Captain Rochefort: The band--the chaps who toot the horns. And personnel said, "What are you going to do with these people?" I said, "I'll take them." So I took the band. They were pretty good as a matter of fact.

Q: They at least could read music, so they could read everything perhaps? Was that your thought or were they just men available?

Rochefort - 121

Captain Rochefort: No, they were men available at that stage. Somebody told me once that they picked up a kid and I think this kid had been sealed in--now this must have been the Arizona or it could have been the Oklahoma, which capsized. It was one of those two ships. And he had been sealed in and lost for a couple of days and they finally get this kid out from underwater. The kid was pretty well shaken up, as I remember. He looked to me like he was about 16 or 17 years old. And this would be a horrible experience for a kid.

Q: For anybody.

Captain Rochefort: So they wanted to know if I would take this kid off their hands, and I said, "Sure, I'll take him off your hands." So I sent him out to one of our little stations on the far side of the island with a little note to the chief radioman, "Let this kid lay in the sand or the grass or something out at your place and let him stare at the sky for a couple or three days and then when you think he's ready for it, then put him to work." Eventually he came back to our place and turned out to be all right. It was quite an experience. But I told the chief just to keep him there for a week or so.

Q: That was a kindly thing to do.

Captain Rochefort: Well, I really felt sorry for him. He had apparently been in some compartment or something and got sealed in.

Q: Probably everybody else was dead around him.

Captain Rochefort: By the grace of God, they got this kid out of there. So we just dumped him out in one of our outlying stations and let him lay in the sand and look at the sky and the sun. But he came out all right. He made out all right.

Q: You're described by Lord as "tall, thin and humorously caustic."*

Captain Rochefort: I got a big kick out of that. I don't know where he ever dug that up, no more than the smoking jacket or the felt slippers.

Q: Of course, I was going to ask you about that too.

Captain Rochefort: Well, what actually happened there was, on December 7th my family was still living on Oahu Avenue back of the University, and I spent all of my time

---

*Walter Lord referred to Rochefort in his book Incredible Victory (New York: Harper & Row, 1967).

Rochefort - 123

out at the office. I'd come home every third or fourth or fifth day or something like that and get sort of cleaned up. Then we got our family out at the first opportunity. When that happened, I just moved out to the navy yard in one of the houses out there which, by this time most of the families had gone, just leaving the officers there. So I was invited by the planning officer to live in a house where he was and that was my home then for the rest of the period. During this period, of course, I'd spend all of the time in the office, putting in around 20 or 22 hours a day, I would say.

Q: All of you?

Captain Rochefort: No. Just about six of us, I guess. Six of us would just stay there. I would only leave when I had to leave and that was just about all. The rest of the kids would sit on the watch and watch, 12 on and 12 off, because they wouldn't be accustomed to this thing. Well anyway, we had--to go back just a little bit--we had just moved into these new quarters of ours down in the basement. The office was down in the basement of the administration building, and it was being built particularly for us, and it was about completed, say, 1 December. It was just about being completed, so we hastily moved in there before December 7th, and we were down in that place on December 7th. This was just the basement. Actually we only had one door in it. No door out except one door; that was the only way you could get in or out of that place. It was all right. We moved in there, but we didn't have a chance to check a lot of the systems like the air conditioning system. We noticed gradually as we went along, along about January or February or March of '42, there was an awful lot of colds and sniffles and one thing. So we began to check on this, and the first thing you know, we're all coughing and hacking. And after this went on for about a month or so, I told one fellow that I could least spare at that moment--that I could spare not for too much time--to check on this thing for me. He discovered that there wasn't any air conditioning. We were living down there for two months, and it simply wasn't there--there was no fresh air. When we took care of that, then our problem sort of eased up. The air conditioning when it was installed, all it was doing was churning the same air around. This had been going on and we didn't have time to fiddle around with this thing or even ask why. Instead of that we were all chewing these goof balls.

Q: Stay with no-doze pills.

Captain Rochefort: All that no-doze and junk like that. Dyer had buckets full of pills sitting on his desk, and every so often he would just grab a couple and put them in his mouth. And this went on for about 48 hours at a stretch. So it was a very fantastic operation down there.

I started to wear a smoking jacket over the uniform and I wore this darn thing because it had pockets in it and I could get my pipe and my pouch this way. Then my feet got sore. It was from the concrete floor we had down there. That's all we had--a concrete floor. And my feet kept getting sore. So I started wearing slippers because the shoes hurt my feet. So I started wearing slippers and this is where Lord gets the story.

Q: He must have talked to someone who worked in the unit.

Captain Rochefort: He must have talked to somebody, and that must have impressed this person, whoever it was.

Q: Well, it is an interesting item. I was going to ask you was it true. But you see, you make account of it, you see, that he doesn't make, which is that you wore it over your uniform.

Captain Rochefort: Oh yes, I wore it over my uniform. It was a sort of reddish smoking jacket that somebody had given me. The main reason for wearing it besides keeping me warm was that it had pockets where I could keep my pouch and pipe.

Q: But he doesn't make the point that you wore it over your uniform which, to a Navy person, is really a different atmosphere. This is like you say the Japanese translations-- it's a tiny thing but to somebody who is aware of the uniform and so on...

Captain Rochefort: The reason for it was very simple. It wasn't that I was eccentric or anything.

Q: No, it was perfectly obvious when you say it.

Captain Rochefort: It was a practical matter, and I was just cold. Of course, we were wearing khaki all the time--that was all everybody was wearing, khaki. And I was probably just cold, so I developed this idea of wearing this thing. If I had to go outside, of course, I'd put my hat on but very rarely did I go outside except for lunch or rarely for breakfast or something like that. And he also comments on the confusion that existed there.

Q: I was going to ask you about that. Yes, he said things were just knee-deep practically and that you'd go--first, before you go on that, can you describe what the office--how it was furnished, how large it was, and did you have desks, tables--did you work standing up, did you work sitting down or what?

Captain Rochefort: Most of the people worked sitting down. We just had desks. It was a flat open area and it was the basement of a building--I'll have to guess now, I'd say maybe 40, 50 or 60 feet in one direction and maybe a couple hundred feet in the other.

Q: Oh, a great area?

Captain Rochefort: Oh yes. And then later we expanded this. We kicked out a wall and expanded this into another area, and I moved into that because there would be less racket in there and there would be no sound from this other place. And I moved in there and that was my place. All I had with me then was Jasper Holmes.* He used to take care of the charts and the maps. But just very--nothing in the place at all except you would probably find a tremendous amount of IBM cards in their little boxes, like so--oh, maybe a couple of million of those. We used two or three million of those in a month.

Q: What did you use those for?

Captain Rochefort: Our whole operation depended on IBM machines. We were way ahead of anybody else. The IBM

---

*Lieutenant Wilfred J. Holmes, USN, who later discussed Rochefort at length in his book Double-Edged Secrets (Annapolis: Naval Institute Press, 1979).

machines being a step between longhand, or typewritten and the computers. You see, we had no computers at that time. So we used IBM cards. As a matter of fact, Dyer installed the first installation that had ever been made. This was Dyer's idea. Without that, we couldn't have done anything.

Q: Can you tell me how that worked?

Captain Rochefort: We'd just assemble the cards and we would be able at any moment then to pick out any group or two or three groups, or half-a-dozen groups, you see, in a message. Suppose the message said, A,B,C,D,E. If we wanted to use this for some reason or another, all we'd tell the officer in charge of this operation, this IBM thing, "Give me all the A,B,C,D,E's you have" and he'd run this whole thing through the collators, through the tabulators, and he would then come up with printed forms where the use of this thing had never been made together with the messages from the groups ahead of it and, of course, after it.

Q: Now who did the key punching to get the material and the IBM cards in the first place?

Captain Rochefort: They were punched by ex-yeomen, people that had been yeomen or yeomen trainees or something like that. They did all the typing.

Q: And where were they getting the information from?

Captain Rochefort: The messages themselves.

Q: They would take a message and...

Captain Rochefort: Copy this all down and from that one message they'd make 60 or 70 cards.

Q: There might be a message with a hundred words in it?

Captain Rochefort: If that were so, it might have about 200 cards from that.

Q: 200 IBM cards to be punched?

Captain Rochefort: Yes, key-punched.

Q: With every group of words or words or whatever and then they would have maybe 200 cards for every message that came in?

Captain Rochefort: They had about 200 cards. If a message contained 100 groups, there might be 200 cards made up.

There would be a minimum of 100 cards. Then these go on what we call a collator or tabulator so we can recall these instantly. And they were all made up into books.

Q: This is the material that came off the tab.

Captain Rochefort: Yes, the things that come off the tabulator.

Q: And was put into books?

Captain Rochefort: Yes, put into books and probably each one of the translators would have his own book and each one of the cryptanalysts would have his book. I didn't bother with these except that I would get the finished product. They would send me the finished product after they were all through with it. And from this finished product then I would have to make the translation.

Q: That was not the decoding.

Captain Rochefort: Oh no.

Q: What did you call that part of the work?

Captain Rochefort: That would be the cryptanalytic business, and the part that I would do then would be the translation.

Q: They would give you a finished message in Japanese, so to speak?

Captain Rochefort: In Japanese--not full. They might have "from Commander-in-Chief Sixth Fleet to Commander-in-Chief, First Striking Force. You will..." And then maybe a bunch of blanks. "Upon completion of this, you will proceed..." and then some more blanks. And my job was to fill that in. I've got to fill those blank sheets in. That's the job, you see, and you get an idea, so you'd say, well...

Q: Well, where would you get your information on what's to fill in the blank?

Captain Rochefort: Because I could remember. I could remember, say, an incident in connection with the Sixth Fleet, which was the submarine fleet. I could remember back maybe three or four months. This fellow sends a similar message to some other command. He sends this. So we dig back in here and produce this from the stack of junk that Walter Lord is talking about. In other words, everything was in my head. Eventually, of course, you've got to get away from this. You've got to get organized. But we didn't have time to get organized.

Rochefort - 132

Q: You would actually remember a previous message of some months past?

Captain Rochefort: Oh Lord, yes, we could remember a hundred of them.

Q: And you would insert that into this other message that was an incoming message?

Captain Rochefort: There would be no problem there. This is one reason why these people are mostly crazy. We'd have no problem at all. You'd mention something and you'd say, "Now wait a minute. Back here when they were around Halmahera on their way down to a landing at Port Something-or-other, there was a message like this. Let's have it." And they'd look in this pile of junk and they were able to locate it.

Q: What do you mean a "pile of junk" really?

Captain Rochefort: All messages, previous messages that had come in.

Q: What would you have them in? A file box?

Captain Rochefort: In my case, it would be laying on the floor.

Q: It really was laying on the floor.

Captain Rochefort: It was stacked up there. You haven't time--you really haven't time to file or cross file or index or cross-index. You just don't have time for this, not when you're using two or three million cards a month. You see, this gets a little bit beyond that.

Q: How many messages would you get in a day, for example? Have you any idea?

Captain Rochefort: Oh, 500 or 1,000.

Q: A day?

Captain Rochefort: Oh yes. I would say that translating at the peak period, which would be probably in the month of May, that I would personally translate about 140 messages a day. And these had probably been previously translated and I was just reviewing them and passing them.

Q: My mind can't grasp what that amounted to.

Captain Rochefort: No, it would take you a considerable period of time to do this, and you can't do this in any eight hours a day. Yes, we would translate a very large number. When I say translate, I mean to fill in as far as we could. And then of course, you'd get a new one here and this leads to another thing over here and this leads to another thing and this is how you fill the whole works up. One letter leads to another and that leads to a third one and so on. Then that's when your memory comes in very handy.

Q: Without it, you would be no value at all.

Captain Rochefort: You couldn't do very much good. We just operated...

Q: Yours was the best memory of all or you wouldn't have been the boss.

Captain Rochefort: No, I don't think that would be necessarily true, but you had the power of recall and you could recall these things, these instances, with no great amount of difficulty. Other people would probably not believe you if you made these statements, but this is how it was done, because we had no machinery other than the IBM. If we had computers and if people knew how to operate them, we would be in business. We wouldn't have to do this.

Q: Is this a proper place to ask you to relate what you were doing on the IBM to what I only know by references to Magic and red and purple machines?

Captain Rochefort: Well, red and purple means they were Japanese cryptographic systems--red and purple, that's what they were related to. The Japanese had had several machines, one of which they called the red--one of them _we_ called the red and one of these _we_ called the purple. These were systems.

Q: But machines.

Captain Rochefort: They were machine-type cipher systems.

Q: That encrypted messages?

Captain Rochefort: They did this by means of machines. This is the machine type of operation. When you're talking about Magic or Ultra, you're talking about the name that we gave these types of communications. If we sent a message over the communications system, either wire or wireless, if this message was composed of information gained or contained or being identical to the Japanese message, we called it Ultra. The Army called it Magic. You're familiar with restricted and confidential and secret.

Rochefort - 136

Q: Yes.

Captain Rochefort: All right. Then top secret, then comes Ultra or we'd have "eyes only" for something like that. We called this type of traffic--we called this Ultra in the Navy and we had our own communications system. We did not use Navy ciphers or anything else. We used our own. All we did was to give our ciphered message to the watch communication officer--we used to call them CWOs, communication watch officers. We would give these messages to those people and we'd say "Transmit." He hasn't the vaguest idea what's in them, and there's no way for him to find out. These were all in our system, using our own machinery and everything else. We called this Ultra. We also had another system which we used for technical things just among ourselves--for very technical discussions. We called this "copek."

Q: I've never heard of that one before.

Captain Rochefort: Then you've probably never heard of one called "khaki." We used these various things. But these were in our own organization.

Q: When you say "our own" you mean your own cryptographic organization.

Captain Rochefort: Communications intelligence--our own communications intelligence organization. So we used the naval communications service to transmit these things.

Rochefort - 138

Interview No. 2 with Captain Joseph J. Rochefort, U.S. Navy(Retired)

Place: Captain Rochefort's home at 420 Via la Soledad, Redondo Beach, California

Date: 21 September 1969

Subject: Biography

Interviewer: Commander Etta-Belle Kitchen, U.S. Navy(Retired)

Q: I am happy to see you again, Captain, and good morning.

Captain Rochefort: Well, thank you very much. I hope you had a pleasant trip up from San Diego.

Q: It was fine, thank you. The last item on the tape--tape one--there was a mention of red and purple machines as it related to encoding, decoding, and in our conversation since I think there was a misunderstanding on my part. Could you clarify that for me or tell me it's not important and let's go on?

Captain Rochefort: I would suggest that the "red" and the "purple" and any other systems of that nature are really not germane and do not deal with the naval operations in the Pacific with which I am somewhat familiar. The machines were, in the first place very technical; secondly in the late Twenties possibly or the early Thirties through the Thirties and, of course, at the outbreak of war they had no further importance insofar as operations in the Pacific were concerned.

I would suggest that we stick to the naval part and leave any discussion regarding the technical part, either the red machine or the purple machine, up to someone else who is possibly more familiar with it. Let us stick to the part of communications and intelligence, particularly at Pearl, that had to do with the operations during '41 to '45.

Q: Fine. You had talked a little bit about your operations in Pearl and just to get off the subject a little bit, I am interested in how many languages you can handle.

Captain Rochefort: We in the Pacific were only interested in the Japanese language, because that was the enemy. It was a prospective enemy prior to December 7th. While we did have people that may or may not have had any proficiency in other foreign languages, they were not essential to our operation. We were only interested in the Japanese side of it.

Q: You interested me last time we talked when you said that one actually didn't need to know the language in order to be able to decode it.

Captain Rochefort: That is true. A cryptanalyst must have a very thorough knowledge of the mechanics of a language and it is not necessary that he, as a cryptanalyst, have any knowledge of the language itself, being able to speak, translate, etc. But it is rather imperative that he know such things as verb endings or all that sort of thing.

Q: Plurals and so on.

Captain Rochefort: Plurals and the various cases and genders of the words in that particular language. You see, to sort of set the stage for this thing, it was decided in the early spring of '41 that we would modify or perhaps maybe reorganize the various parts of communication intelligence in the Navy between Washington, which was then the home office, and the unit at Pearl Harbor, called Hypo, and the unit in Cavite, which was called Cast for "C". We then used to use the things Able, Baker, Cast, Dog, Easy, and Fox and so on.* It was my understanding, and a lot of this was informal between Safford in Washington and myself in Pearl Harbor and whoever was running it in Cavite, as to what our special responsibilities or tasks were, and it was my understanding from a couple of letters that were exchanged between Safford and myself that when

---
*These were the words used for letters in the phonetic alphabet of that period.

I took over the station Hypo in June or July '41, that my job would be the Japanese Navy and specifically the system which we called ***************. Washington would be the general overseer, would back both Hypo and Cast up, because they had more personnel than we had, and they had the facilities that we didn't. And Cast would be more tactical than strategic, because they were on the scene; they were in Cavite. We were somewhat removed in Honolulu, where the atmosphere was perhaps more conducive to being able to work without any pressure. This was my understanding, and accordingly when I took the job over in June of 1941, then I began reorganizing, or let's say I was expanding the station at Hypo from a small research unit into more of an operating unit that could furnish quicker and better information to the commander in chief than possibly Washington could.* And also due to my relationship with Safford who fully appreciated the difficulties, I had a choice of whom I thought would be the most capable people available. They were attached to the Hawaiian unit, and gradually we became more of an operating unit than a research group--still with a basic responsibility of solving the Japanese naval system which we called ***** while presumably Safford and possibly Cavite would continue their work on ***** which was in rather wide use in the Japanese Navy. I presumed

---

*The commander in chief referred to here is Admiral Kimmel of the Pacific Fleet.

that somebody was taking care of the diplomatic traffic, probably Washington in conjunction with the Army, and somebody was taking care of the Japanese Army traffic, presumably the U.S. Army. But I was not particularly interested in either one of these projects because it was not assigned to me. I assumed that somebody else was taking care of it which, of course, they were. In any event, we had not gotten ourselves fully organized except for the minor Japanese naval systems on which we continued to furnish the commander in chief the information on as best we could. One of the prime defects in the Pacific as far as I was concerned was the operation of the DF net, the direction-finder net, and we devoted a great deal of attention to making it more operational than it had been so that we could locate Japanese units with a greater degree of precision than we were able to do previously. That was the situation as of December 7th.

Then shortly after December 7th, as I recall, I was informed by Safford that station Hypo had been given a new task which was the solution of ****************************
****
***.

Q: Was that the one the Japs were using at the time of Pearl Harbor?

Captain Rochefort: Yes, and this was perhaps the most important system, in that it contained most of the operational

information and directives, operational orders, etc., etc.
As I recall, just in passing, we were never able to do
anything with *************, not to my knowledge. Anyway,
we immediately then concentrated all of our efforts on
****** and gradually Hypo, because of the additional personnel
and because of the pressure in Pearl Harbor and possibly,
I like to think so anyway, possibly because of our greater
competence in Pearl, we gradually took the lead on the
solution, although there was a free exchange of information
between the people at Cavite and Pearl Harbor and Washington.
There was always a free exchange of information at the
technical side. This, of course, immediately produced
results to the end that possibly by January and February
we were well into the breaking process, being assisted
by the people at Cavite and in Washington. Although Cavite
at this time was in the throes of being moved out, and
they had to gradually proceed down into Australia to Bellconner,
and this was called Bell--we always referred to this as
Bell. It was in Australia. I would say that by possibly
March we were able to glean a considerable amount of
information from the traffic until we were able to form
a judgment in our minds as to what the Japanese overall
plan was, of the individual operations such as Coral Sea,
Midway, and so on. Although we still hadn't, you might
say, solved the system itself. We were able to get a
considerable amount of information from the traffic. We

were able to guess with fair degree of accuracy as to what the Japanese plans of operation were. Does that answer your question?

Q: Yes, and it does set the stage within which we can get more detail.

Captain Rochefort: Yes, for what happened later. I think, as I've described to you before, my views on the duties of a communications intelligence person or the cryptanalyst or the translator or the officer in charge of such a section I think are far different than the normal concept of this. It so happened that I had been involved in the fleet during the latter part of the Twenties and into the Thirties in the fleet operations and had extensive duty including assistant fleet operations officer and temporary duty as fleet operations officer. I had served as intelligence officer as well as the normal ship duty, and I considered that I was perhaps fairly well fitted to render a judgment on what the Japanese intended than the average intelligence officer because of my staff training and duties on the staff of Commander in Chief United States Fleet, Battle Force, Scouting Force, and shore establishments. Therefore, the estimates that came from Station Hypo were not the estimates of technical people such as cryptanalysts or language officers or translators or communications intelligence people. They were the considered opinions of people who had this capability as well as having had the experience of serving in the operations department of the various staffs in the fleet. Of course, I've indicated before I was also a translator, having served three years in Tokyo as a language officer, and I felt that I had the knowledge and experience of being able to estimate and form a judgment on what the traffic actually meant, because we were not able to read the thing completely anyway, and all we would get would be fragments. With the people that I had out there that were equally capable, we had a small group there, say three or four or five, who could not only analyze what the Japanese were saying but also would come up with a very good solution or estimate of the situation which other people probably would not have this knowledge and experience.

Q: Were the people for whom you were working--say, the intelligence officer on the staff of CinCPacFleet--willing to accept this estimate? What was their reaction or attitude toward you and your estimate?

Captain Rochefort: This was perhaps one of the more awkward cases. The fleet intelligence officer, Lieutenant Commander Layton, was a close personal friend of mine. We had spent three years in Japan together, and I had worked with him on several occasions subsequent to that, and although I did not have direct access to Admiral Nimitz, which I think would have been preferable, I had to go through Layton because he was the fleet intelligence officer. But I think our relationship--that is, between Layton and myself--was such that he and I understood each other's problems, and I would put these messages on the air for Commander in Chief Pacific and CominCh, I also discussed them in great detail with Layton.

Q: What do you mean you put this on the air?

Captain Rochefort: I put them on the radio.

Q: To him?

Captain Rochefort: To CominCh and CinCPac.

Q: Weren't you in the same building?

Captain Rochefort: No, no. Layton was with commander in chief, who operated from the submarine base at Pearl and then later up to Makalapa headquarters. I was always in the 14th Naval District. My orders actually specifically read for duty with the Commandant 14th Naval District. He was my immediate superior. But he was very understanding and allowed me to deal directly with Layton. I always kept Layton informed of what we had and what we were doing.

And of course, he being a language officer was extremely helpful also. He and I would discuss these little language difficulties on occasion. Layton's main problem was to coordinate my activities together with his other bits of information that he might have, either from prisoners of war or from Washington or from some other place. Whereas I was only concerned with the elements of crypanalytic attack and the translation and evaluation which I always furnished Layton. It was a rather awkward situation, but during my time out there we never had any difficulty due to our close personal relationship.

Q: But your contact with this was through radio?

Captain Rochefort: Oh no.

Q: You said, "I would put it on the air."

Captain Rochefort: I'd put it on the air then, either before that or after that, I would call Layton and tell him that I'm putting something on the air and he would see this thing and would understand the background. But he was physically removed by a mile, I suppose, and of course, he and I talked possibly two or three times a day over the telephone. Occasionally we would get together and discuss some particular problem. The organization

Rochefort - 148

was not particularly good in that they had me here and ostensibly under the command of Com 14, where Layton was under the command of CinCPac. As I said, our personal relationship was such that there was no problem particularly involved in it as long as Layton was where he was and I was where I was.

Q: But did they accept your evaluations, or was it Layton then taking your estimates and transmitting it to Admiral Nimitz?

Captain Rochefort: Yes, Layton had to transmit my estimates to Nimitz. Now, he may or may not, because this was no concern of mine. The matter didn't concern me. I didn't become involved in it. Layton may or may not have given his own evaluation based on other information he had available. He may have done this. In any event, my evaluations, having gone out in official messages or dispatches, were official and this was my feeling.

Q: And they were in code, of course.

Captain Rochefort: Oh, yes. We had our own cipher system so that nobody, not even the communication watch officers could read these things. This was in our own particular private system which was not available to anybody else in the Navy. I mention this organization, because in the future I think it would be better to try to avoid denigrating these communications intelligence people, these cryptanalysts and the translators and the radio intelligence personnel, the direction finder personnel and all the specialized intelligence. These people should be trained in fleet operations or naval operations in order that they can better perform their job. This was the great weakness in Washington.

Q: Wouldn't it have been easier had you been attached to CinCPac's staff, to Admiral Nimitz's own staff and located closer to him?

Captain Rochefort: I was later. Some minor question came up, I think, with somebody on CinCPac's staff and I said, "Don't tell me about your problems. I'm working for Com 14." So they immediately had me transferred to extra duty with Admiral Nimitz.

Q: Just orders. Not location. Not geographic.

Captain Rochefort: No, I was ordered so that I would be under, if necessary, under more direct control of Admiral Nimitz. Although this was not at all necessary. But I don't think that the organization was possibly the best that could be devised.

Q: Did you ever make any written recommendations about that?

Captain Rochefort: No, no. This was presumably the way Admiral Nimitz wanted it.

Q: Of course, he inherited what was there when he came.

Captain Rochefort: Yes, but previously, you see, to the best of my knowledge, no one else had ever taken this step of some specialized little intelligence organization, not only giving their intelligence estimates but also going farther in rendering a judgment and making an estimate of the entire situation.

Q: Evaluate and estimate and interpret and so on.

Captain Rochefort: No one had done this before.

Q: A forecast, really.

Captain Rochefort: Yes, and also make long-range forecasts. I did this, because I was convinced that in the personnel in Hypo that we had the personnel who were best fitted to perform this duty in that they were all experienced, they were all knowledgeable, they had some 5, 10, and in some cases 15 years' experience in doing this. We had the unique opportunity there of having this particular group that I was extremely proud of and I considered it a privilege to be with.

Q: You had selected them, had you not?

Captain Rochefort: I had selected all of these people myself. They were all personal friends.

Q: Now you've mentioned this Jasper Holmes and you've mentioned Dyer. What was his first name?

Captain Rochefort: Tommy. Ham Wright.

Q: And yourself, that's four.

Captain Rochefort: Then we had a radio intelligence organization. We had Jack Williams and Tom Huckins in the traffic part or radio intelligence part, direction finders in the specialized units.

Q: That was six of you?

Captain Rochefort: Yes, and as one of the translators we had Joe Finnegan and Fullinwider--he had two or three brothers on active duty--this was Ransom Fullinwider. These people were particularly outstanding.

Q: And was this the group that worked as often as sometimes 10, 15, 20, 22 hours a day?

Captain Rochefort: That would be the normal. Normal would be possibly 20 hours a day. In the days immediately preceding, say, Coral and Midway, it would be unusual to have these people put in less than 20 hours a day.

Q: I don't know how they existed.

Captain Rochefort: Pills, pills.

Q: Where did they get the pills? At the dispensary?

Captain Rochefort: I would presume so. I would never ask.

Q: Did you take pills?

Captain Rochefort: No, no. I dislike any form of pills. But I would say 20 hours a day would be quite normal for those people. The rest of them were watch and watch.

Rochefort - 153

Q: The things I have read led me to believe that your office was in the same building with Admiral Nimitz.

Captain Rochefort: Oh no.

Q: Now you have clarified it, and will you tell me again where it was in the building and how large it was and describe the lighting and the heating.

Captain Rochefort: In the old administration building in 14th Naval District which was, as I recall, a two-story buidling with a small basement and a balcony on the second deck. When I went over there first, we were on the second deck in several rooms off this balcony, and we immediately proceeded to make arrangements for moving into the basement, which was then enlarged to take care of us. In fact, without realizing it, this was probably the first bomb shelter we had in 14th Naval District. This was done completely unintentionally. They enlarged the basement, as I recall, and put in an air conditioning unit and so on and made it completely separate and distinct from the rest of the structure with its own entrance and its own exit.

Q: How did you get in?

Captain Rochefort: We got in through a door at the ground

level and went downstairs to the basement. That then became our place.

Q: And people had to go through two doors?

Captain Rochefort: Yes, as I recall--I didn't pay too much attention to these details. These I left up to the chief yeoman that we had that was quite capable of getting the things we wanted, and I never inquired where he got them or anything else. He produced these things from somewhere, being a good chief petty officer.

Q: And how did people get in? Did they have a password, a badge or identification?

Captain Rochefort: No, we had the thing usually locked. We had the thing locked, and then we had some desks at the immediate entrance in the basement, so it was impossible to get through or by these desks without the people seeing them, and anybody that wasn't known, of course, just didn't enter.

Q: Know them personally?

Captain Rochefort: Yes, they had to be known personally. We never went for too much security details in the best tradition of cops and robbers, because it wasn't necessary. Nobody came in without our knowledge. Let's just leave it at that--nobody came in without our knowledge, and people that were not welcome or not considered safe to be in there, then they were stopped at the door. But we never had that problem.

Q: What color were the walls painted?

Captain Rochefort: Oh I think some kind of a dun color or beige or some standard Navy color.

Q: Were the lights fluorescent lights?

Captain Rochefort: I couldn't tell you. I couldn't remember that. They were adequate; that was all I know. Unfortunately, during this period when we were moving in was before and after December 7th. So this, of course--whatever steps we were taking about fixing up the office, we were never able to do this because December 7th intervened. We forgot this stuff immediately.

Q: And you were a mile, you say, from the commander in chief's office.

Captain Rochefort: I would say--it was in the administration building of the 14th Naval District which was rather adjacent, not too far from the old dock--Ten Ten Dock.* I would say possibly a mile over to submarine headquarters, possibly a mile.

Q: And your office was furnished with tables and desks.

Captain Rochefort: Just tables and desks. I don't even remember at this stage of the game what they were. They were nothing particular.

Q: Plus some IBM equipment?

Captain Rochefort: We had IBM equipment in one of the other rooms.

Q: You told me you didn't have a computer, and you said that if we had had a computer our job would have been much easier.

Captain Rochefort: Oh yes.

Q: Why didn't you have a computer?

---

*Ten Ten Dock--part of the Pearl Harbor Navy Yard, so named because it was 1,010 feet long.

Rochefort - 157

Captain Rochefort: Because they hadn't been invented. It's that simple. This is 1941.

Q: You're speaking of just a regular present-day computer.

Captain Rochefort: Oh yes, we never had that--it was possibly in some of the universities or engineering schools, but they were not in general use. We were fortunate, because we were using IBM cards, which was a tremendous help.

Q: You had the key punch for the cards, and you had a collator and a tabulator.

Captain Rochefort: We were using--to give you an idea of the scope of the operation--we were using, I would say, from the spring of '42 on, at least several million IBM cards a month.

Q: You told me that you got 500 to 1,000 messages a day, and out of each of those messages you would make x number of cards for every message, so I can imagine. You also said that Dyer was the one who devised...

Captain Rochefort: He devised this system, and he installed it in Washington quite a few years before the Army took it over. I would say in the early Thirties, although I was not in Washington at the time. He conceived this idea, realizing that as time goes on we were not going to be able to do this thing longhand anymore at all.

Q: Or a typewriter either.

Captain Rochefort: Or a typewriter--you couldn't do this at all. So we had to have some rapid form of digesting the information, and the only thing on the market at that time was the IBM which we could use.

Q: I hate to refer to this magic and purple machine, but in the amount of material I've been able to read, one book implied--and I can't tell you what book it was--that had there been "a purple machine at Pearl Harbor it would have made a difference on December 7th" and implied that the machines were given deliberately to England and one out to Cavite but not to you.

Captain Rochefort: Much has been made of this, and my reply has always been the same--that is, what difference would it have made? We were assigned a task which involved only systems used by the Japanese Navy. We were given some material on some consular codes and ciphers and that sort of thing as a sort of a library, and we had people who had worked on these systems, but Washington was undertaking the responsibility of taking care of the diplomatic systems. It was no concern of ours. And if any information was to come to us from Washington regarding information gathered from the diplomatic systems, I would expect Washington to send it--not to me--but to the commander in chief. I did not concern myself with this diplomatic.

Q: And this purple machine does relate to diplomatic traffic.

Captain Rochefort: And only diplomatic traffic. Now if we thought that Washington was not keeping the commander in chief informed, then and if we had had a copy of the purple machine, then, of course, we would have been in a position to have furnished the commander in chief this information. But I saw no necessity for this; in fact, it would have been a little bit disloyal on my part, because the information gleaned from the diplomatic system was being handled in Washington by, I would presume among other people, the State Department, the War Department, the Navy Department, and the President. If they saw anything that the commander in chief should have had, I am sure that my feelings would have been, "All right, they are going to furnish that to him."

Q: But you don't have any feeling that the lack of "that machine" had anything to do with the disaster at Pearl Harbor.

Rochefort - 160

Captain Rochefort: No, no. If we had had that, I am sure that at least Layton and myself could have made a better evaluation of the significance of that traffic than the people in Washington apparently made.

Q: Oh, you do. I think that's significant.

Captain Rochefort: Yes. For example, if we had had a knowledge, I am sure that with Layton's experience and my experience, among others--if we had had copies of those Japanese translations of say November 27th...

Q: That was the ultimatum given?

Captain Rochefort: Yes, the ultimatum. I am sure that we would have told the commander in chief, Admiral Kimmel, our opinion as to what this meant, which was--this means war.

Q: We were going to be attacked, because that was the history of the Japanese, wasn't it?

Captain Rochefort: Well, we built that up. We built these people up to be very nasty people but, in fact, they were just doing the job, that's all.

Q: But I mean in our other wars like the Russo-Japanese and so on.

Captain Rochefort: Well, no known other instances is all.

Q: Only the one other, and that was the Russo-Japanese.

Captain Rochefort: That's all. It only happened once.

Q: In retrospect, can you think that you would have said to him, "We are going to be attacked"?

Captain Rochefort: I'm quite sure that both Layton and I would have attached the proper significance to these messages. I personally did not see these messages until 1944. Now, when Layton saw them or had knowledge of them, I do not know. But I think this matter has been unduly stressed by historians. Even if we had had these messages, all we could have done was to have warned Admiral Kimmel. Whatever action _he_ would have taken would have been based on instructions from Washington.

Q: And they knew it.

Captain Rochefort: And they knew it.

Rochefort - 162

Q: Whether they interpreted it correctly or not is another matter. But Safford was there.

Captain Rochefort: As I say now, this is the difference between somebody like Safford and somebody like, say, Layton or myself.

Q: He is the technician, and you are the technician plus.

Captain Rochefort: That's right. Layton had enough knowledge of cryptanalysis to know about what value to give to this. I was involved in this thing directly, but people in Washington were sort of compartmented and you had the cryptanalyst where we might place Safford or these other translators; they were just translators, and that was all. Maybe some of them had never been on a ship. I would say that if we had had a purple machine, and if we had had copies of these intercepts--which I could have arranged to get through the cable companies or the radio companies. I doubt whether we would have devoted a great deal of effort, because, as I've said before, this was the function of Washington. Washington was doing this. There isn't any point in other people doing it.

Q: But do you think you would have told Admiral Kimmel, "Here are these messages and here's what I think they mean"?

Captain Rochefort: Yes, I'm sure that both Layton and I would have done this because of our knowledge of the Japanese. But I do not attach any particular significance to the non-receipt of a purple machine by station Hypo.

Q: There's an impression that it was done deliberately.

Captain Rochefort: This may or may not be. I do not know.

Q: You've read, of course.

Captain Rochefort: I've read these things.

Q: Indicating that Roosevelt did it deliberately so that the people would be unified and that we would go to war and so on.

Captain Rochefort: Well, this implies that Mr. Roosevelt was something other than loyal.

Q: It sounds terrible.

Captain Rochefort: I would not accept this.

Q: I am happy to hear you say it, because when I read it--and you don't read it once. If you look through the books, you see it referred to not infrequently. It would just be such a horrible thing.

Captain Rochefort: He may have for his own reasons decided that the policy of this country required that we be at war with either Japan or Germany. This may have been his judgment on the whole matter. Not having ever met Mr. Roosevelt, I am not in a position to say what was in his mind. But if he did, then this would be considered a very serious error in judgment. But you say that he deliberately kept this information from the fleet commanders. This is a little bit too broad, I think. I would not be willing to go this far.

Q: The first time I read it, I was just horrified, and I thought maybe I was naive and hadn't known what happened in history.

Captain Rochefort: He may have been misinformed; he may have been given poor advice; he may have decided that it was imperative for the future that the United States be in a war with either Germany or Japan or both. He may have decided this. I'm in no position to say what he decided. But in any event, whether or not we had the purple machine physically present in Pearl Harbor would not have materially altered any decisions or actions that were made at Pearl Harbor.

Rochefort - 165

Q: Except for the one thing that you said, that you would have been able to interpret it.

Captain Rochefort: We could have said that ourselves, yes.

Q: But what would have happened to it is anybody's guess.

Captain Rochefort: Well, Admiral Kimmel then would have had to try to make a decision as to what he was going to do with the fleet and, at that point, as you possibly will recall, we had insufficient air units to conduct a complete air search from Pearl to a reasonable distance of 500 or 600 miles, which was considered at that time to be what was required. That is, if you had airplanes on the circumference of a circle 600 miles radius from Pearl Harbor at, say, sundown, then the carriers or ship-borne planes could not arrive to make an attack on Pearl Harbor prior to daylight the next morning at which point we would then have an inner search of 100 miles at daylight out, so we'd be fully protected. We did not have the airplanes to make the search. These airplanes were being diverted--these would be the PBY types, the B-24s--these planes were being diverted to other places in the Atlantic which were probably or possibly considered of greater importance.* It's just as simple as that.

---

*PBYs were long-range Navy patrol planes; B-24s were long-range Army Air Forces bombers.

Rochefort - 166

Q: Did the Japanese send out any fake radio signals or messages to deceive deliberately?

Captain Rochefort: No, no. This is another matter that has been built up by some sensation-seekers.

Q: Well, you know, Lord speaks of it.

Captain Rochefort: Yes, and this originated in the minds of apparently some such people as Commander Redman, who was something less than capable or competent.

Q: He was one of the men you referred to as wanting to expand the empire for his own personal aggrandizement?

Captain Rochefort: Yes, this is my opinion. But to the best of my knowledge, against a trained counter-communications intelligence organization like, say, communications security, it is awfully difficult to deceive them, awfully difficult.

Q: When I read that, it jarred me to thinking a little bit out of key, off key, because from what you had talked to me about, I couldn't believe that you hadn't been able to identify it.

Captain Rochefort: No, I do not think radio deception in the Pacific would have been successful against our own operators

Rochefort - 167

in the field and against our own officer personnel such as Huckins and Williams. I do not think so. I've been informed that in the Atlantic several such things were tried both by us and by the Germans, and in all instances these were unsuccessful. But I have no particular knowledge of this.

Q: Did you ever intercept any messages that were being sent from the mainland, that is from Pearl Harbor, out to Japanese? Say, a civilian on Pearl Harbor--did they ever send any messages out to the Japanese by way of treasonous actions that you ever knew about or did you ever intercept it?

Captain Rochefort: No, much has been said about one of the Japanese vice consuls who was supposed to have transmitted a lot of the traffic relative to American vessels moored in Pearl Harbor at various times. This was not the first instance that this was ever done, nor will it be the last.

Q: Well, he was a consul anyway. I meant from a civilian spy, so to speak.

Captain Rochefort: No, we had no such thing in Pearl Harbor. I recall once I attended a meeting which I think I asked for, and this meeting was attended by the Army security people, G-2, and by, among other people, the district intelligence officer, Captain Mayfield, and I attended this meeting.* During the course of this meeting, I recall asking the FBI agent in charge did he know of any specific instances of Japanese spying or illegal operations? And he told me, no. And he would, of course, be the person who was best informed.

Q: I would think he'd be in the best position to know.

Captain Rochefort: His name was Bob Shivers, and I had met with him before the war. But there has been much written and said about Japanese spying activities along the island. I would say that these were not in excess of what our own people might do in different circumstances. It was just normal information gathering regarding the number of ships in port and when they proceeded out and their procedure in leaving port and arriving and so on. This is just standard practice; this was not spying.

Q: Did the fact that the Japanese code was shifted, changed just before Pearl Harbor, about the 1st of December, give you any clue that something was afoot?

Captain Rochefort: Yes, we knew this, but, as I explained before, possibly to other people, in my opinion, we were

---

*Captain Irving H. Mayfield, USN, intelligence officer on the staff of the Commandant, 14th Naval District.

convinced--I say "we," I mean people around Pearl Harbor who were presumably competent to discuss these things--that certainly the Japanese were going to move, and they were going to move very shortly. But I think our reasoning went something like this: if the Japanese moved against the United States, say, either at Manila or at Pearl Harbor, then this means war, as the Japanese are well aware of what's going to result here. If we become involved in a war with Japan, the Japanese cannot possibly win; therefore, the Japanese will not proceed against the United States directly but will rather reach their goals by, say, toward possibly Singapore, certainly Southeast Asia, maybe some of the islands but not the Philippines because this would probably bring them to war. Therefore, they will then proceed along the Asiatic mainland, which they were in the process of doing, and might possibly move against New Guinea and possibly move against the Malay Archipelago but certainly not against the United States.

Q: Mainland.

Captain Rochefort: Yes. This was an unfortunate attitude, but I think that this would be a fair appraisal of the thinking at least at Pearl.

Q: Although you did know something was afoot.

Captain Rochefort: We knew, of course, that there was going to be a major operation or operations. We knew this, but I think most people assumed, and certainly the people in the Asiatic Fleet subscribed to the same theory and apparently the people in Washington subscribed to the same theory--that the Japanese would move to reach their goal, which was what is now called Indonesia and that general area, without proceeding directly against the United States. And it is very doubtful that the United States would react under a situation like that.

Q: You said in the last interview that it was better that the ships were all in Pearl Harbor anyway.

Captain Rochefort: Yes, as it turned out, the Japanese made two fatal mistakes. In the first place, they started a war which they were bound to lose and which even the Japanese knew that.

Q: Don't you think that they intended to start a war?

Captain Rochefort: No, I didn't say that. I said, they started a war which they knew at the time they couldn't win.

Q: But they knew they were starting a war.

Captain Rochefort: Oh yes, they knew this. It was one of these things that people familiar with the Japanese mentality might understand, but the average person wouldn't. But what else was there for the Japanese to do?

Q: Well, after these ultimatums, you did explain that last time.

Captain Rochefort: Yes, so what could they do?

Q: One of their fatal errors was starting a war they couldn't win.

Captain Rochefort: And they knew this. And the second was that when they attacked the people at Pearl, rather than attack the installations, they attacked the ships. If they had attacked the installations and had done a comparable job--I'm speaking now of the navy yard establishment, the dry docks, the fuel oil, the storage, which we had been gradually building up thanks to Mr. Doheny and Mr. Albert Fall, then we would possibly have had to go back to San Francisco and start from there.[*]

Q: It is odd, isn't it, that they just attacked the ships?

---

[*] Edward Doheny and Albert Fall were two individuals involved in the Teapot Dome scandal over naval oil reserves during the Harding Administration.

Rochefort - 172

Captain Rochefort: They were under the same misapprehension as we were--that the battleships were the most important targets.

Q: That was, of course, the same thinking in both navies at that time, too.

Captain Rochefort: Yes, the battleships were the most important target.

Q: Aside from the terrible loss of life, as a matter of fact, it was probably a favor in a way to fight a war, bringing the carriers into a position where they would not have otherwise been placed, I'm sure, if the battleships hadn't been destroyed.

Captain Rochefort: Yes, it was one of those things that worked out to our advantage. I remember a statement made by Admiral Standley, who was a member of the Roberts commission, when they reviewed the damage about the 10th or 15th or so of December.* When they viewed the damage and asked how many people were lost, he was told 2,000 or 3,000, and his reply after some thinking was, this was a pretty cheap price to pay for unifying the country.

---

*Chaired by Supreme Court Justice Owen Roberts, the commission was appointed by President Roosevelt shortly after the Japanese attack to investigate the causes for the fleet being caught by surprise.

Q: That's, of course, the kind of remark that makes you kind of freeze when you hear it.

Captain Rochefort: Yes, it was a pretty cheap price to pay for unifying the country. Which I would fully subscribe to, actually.

Q: Well, now to go on from Pearl, in your setting the stage, you mentioned the fact that your mission was shifted after the 7th.

Captain Rochefort: Yes.

Q: Then the next event in which history speaks of the development of your unit was the alert and the information received from the Japanese intercepted messages of how it affected the Battle of the Coral Sea. As a matter of fact, before this Battle of Coral Sea was the time when you heard directly from Admiral King?*

Captain Rochefort: As I recall, it was either during or immediately after the so-called attack in the Indian Ocean by the same units that had been at Pearl on December 7th, which we referred to as Kido Butai, which was the Japanese striking force for want of a better definition, which was

---

*Admiral Ernest J. King, USN, Commander in Chief U.S. Fleet (CominCh).

composed of the carriers and the supporting destroyers. Butai meaning a detachment or a unit or a squadron or a force or something of that type; kido meaning striking or forcing. So we referred to it always as a striking force.

Shortly after their operations in the Indian Ocean, I received, as I recall, a message from CominCh asking for Station Hypo's estimate of further Japanese or future Japanese intentions.

Q: Did that come to you as officer in charge? Or to you, Rochefort?

Captain Rochefort: No, it came to me as the officer in charge from CominCh, and we had several meetings with my people, as I recall. We finally drafted a message of reply with an information copy to CinCPac, who had also received an information copy of this message from CominCh. Generally, the following evaluation: that (a) the operations in the Indian Ocean were concluded and the units were now returning to their Japanese home bases. Secondly, there was another operation planned in the vicinity of eastern New Guinea, which had for its intention to secure the eastern end of New Guinea for the Japanese. It later developed into the Coral Sea. That the Japanese had no intention of invading Australia. And that, fourth, that there was another operation that was being planned for the future, and we had no information to furnish at this time, other than that it was an operation different and distinct from the operation planned off New Guinea and was to be in the Pacific, of course, and it was a major operation involving most of the units of the Japanese fleet. This later turned out to be Midway. As I say, the time of this was, I thought, in late March, possibly in early April but in any event subsequent to the attacks in the Indian Ocean.

Q: Yes, and prior to the Coral Sea. So that would be March or April, probably.

Captain Rochefort: This was generally the first information we had on Midway, and it was gleaned from a general regrouping of the Japanese fleet units.

Q: How many hours did it take you to make this evaluation?

Captain Rochefort: Oh, a matter of six or eight hours.

Q: And all of you working together?

Captain Rochefort: This was the combined opinion of possibly six of us, of which I was responsible. I had the responsibility for this.

Rochefort - 176

Q: Would you say that Admiral King acted on it?

Captain Rochefort: I have no way of knowing. I did get a negative response from one or two members of Admiral Nimitz's staff who considered that making such an estimate was their responsibility and not mine.

Q: Who were they?

Captain Rochefort: Several members--oh, let's say the least competent members of the people that we had had who were not particularly appreciative of, they said, me taking over their functions, which was true.

Q: Who were they? Do you remember their names?

Captain Rochefort: Yes, there was a Vincent Murphy, that I think was in planning.[*] I don't believe anyone else such as Admiral Draemel or Admiral McMorris, because I had several personal discussions with both of those admirals.[**]

Q: Draemel?

Captain Rochefort: Draemel, first name, Milo.

---
[*] Captain Vincent R. Murphy, USN.
[**] Rear Admiral Milo F. Draemel, USN; Captain Charles H. McMorris, USN.

Rochefort - 177

Q: Did you have any reaction from Admiral Nimitz or Layton on this message?

Captain Rochefort: No, I don't recall Layton bringing up the subject. He must have, but I don't recall. If he did, it would probably be in a joking fashion.

Q: How did you react when you got this message from Admiral King?

Captain Rochefort: We were a little surprised that he would ask us what our views were. I personally felt that he was not even aware of our existence.

Q: Up to that time?

Captain Rochefort: Up to that point.

Q: I wonder who advised him that you could give him this type of estimate?

Captain Rochefort: I don't know.

Q: Haven't you often wondered?

Captain Rochefort: I've wondered about this, but certainly

Rochefort - 178

Safford would not have been on those terms with Admiral King.

Q: His boss might have been. Who was that then?

Captain Rochefort: That must have been Admiral Noyes.[*] But I had not known Admiral Noyes. I had not had the privilege of serving with him, so I couldn't tell you. I just don't know how this thing arose. And I was not particularly interested, because obviously at this stage of the game we had other things to be concerned about such as, at that time, Coral Sea and later on Midway. So we didn't have any time to discuss this.

Q: You didn't sit around and think about that anyway.

Captain Rochefort: We didn't have any sort of a bull session, no, certainly not. It just came and went, and that was it.

Q: There was something else more exciting or pressing to take its place, I am sure.

Captain Rochefort: We had other things to do rather than wondering about that sort of thing.

---

[*] Rear Admiral Leigh Noyes, USN, Director of Naval Communications.

Q: It would be interesting in history, however, to go back to find out what prompted him to get that direct contact, which is certainly unusual.

Captain Rochefort: Yes, I don't recall whether he also asked Station Cast or it was then probably Bell. Bellconner. I don't recall whether he asked them or not. I don't recall much about it other than the message itself in which we were asked to make an estimate, and which we did and there was an unfavorable reaction from one or two people on the CinCPac staff.

Q: You named Vince Murphy. Do you remember the name of the other one?

Captain Rochefort: No, I don't because I am sure the planning people over there, Delany.[*] It would not have been, of course, Admiral McMorris. He was a close personal friend of mine, as was Admiral Draemel, who had been in my office on quite a few occasions just discussing the overall situation. So I don't know. It was somebody junior. It didn't make any difference.

Q: ***?

Captain Rochefort: ****************************.

---

[*] Captain Walter Delany, USN.

Rochefort - 180

Q: **********************?

Captain Rochefort: **************************************.

Q: How did you go about getting that information to the operations people? Was that by message to Layton, who passed it on? I'm just curious about the routine that went on.

Captain Rochefort: No, you see, we made as a sort of a daily routine--we would make daily reports to the fleet intelligence officer in the form of just a sort of overall, what we thought was the overall happenings, particularly of the future, in addition to which Jasper Holmes also presented a daily plot of all Japanese ship positions which I believe he furnished to Layton. I never paid too much attention to this actually. This was between Jasper Holmes and Layton just as a service to the fleet intelligence officer. Then insofar as traffic was concerned, if we had any translations or partial translations of any value, which we thought would have value, then we usually went on the air on radio, and they were sent to Admiral Nimitz just officially through the ordinary channels and to CominCh, Admiral King. Now who back there handled them, I have no way of knowing. Then the technical traffic was handled as it occurred on our own systems between either Washington, who would be Safford or maybe Bellconner, who would be a lieutenant down there, and

Rochefort - 181

this was more or less technical traffic, exchanging information, recovered values and all that sort of thing.

Q: What kind of values?

Captain Rochefort: Recovered values. This would be what we referred to as technical information.

Q: Then it was Layton's job to get it to the fleet.

Captain Rochefort: No, Layton would not send this to the fleet. At least in the Pacific, this matter was handled in order to provide us with a maximum security, and I'm sure that Layton would have discussed this matter with Admiral Nimitz personally, possibly with the chief of staff or maybe the operations officer, maybe the planning officer. But this would not be generally exchanged even among the CinCPac staff.

Q: Well, how--for example, I just had a talk with Admiral Stroop, and he was the intelligence officer on the Lexington.* And he said the messages came in and were being decoded and interpreted and were telling them where the Japanese striking force and invading force were coming in to the Coral Sea. Now how did he, Stroop, get that?

Captain Rochefort: Now Stroop did not know where that

---

*Vice Admiral Paul D. Stroop, USN(Ret.), subject of a Naval Institute oral history.

information came from, did he? It might have come from a spy. It might have come from somebody in Tokyo.

Q: It was from traffic.

Captain Rochefort: This is all he knew. But he did not know how far communications intelligence had succeeded. This was the point. In other words, I would give it to Layton. Or rather Layton would receive it, and Layton would act on it, but Layton never, as far as I know, would ever mention our organization.

Q: No, but I wondered how did he get the information, say, to Fletcher who was the overall commander.*

Captain Rochefort: Nimitz would tell Fletcher, for example in the operational...

Q: But not personally.

Captain Rochefort: No, he might have told him personally when Fletcher was, say, in Pearl Harbor. He might have told him personally with the instructions that he is not to pass this information on to anyone. In other words, it doesn't make any difference where you get the information.

---

*Rear Admiral Frank Jack Fletcher, USN, task force commander for the Midway operation.

If you say, "I have information to the effect that tomorrow the French, the Germans, the British, or somebody else are going to take some particular action," you do not have to indicate the source of your information.

Q: But he implied that there were messages coming in constantly that had to be evaluated.

Captain Rochefort: That's true. But he never got any translations of Japanese messages. All he got was the information contained in them. For example, Nimitz. If you recall, Walter Lord says in his book that Nimitz just got his people together and he says, "I have information to the effect that such and such a thing is going to happen. This is what we are going to do." But Nimitz never indicated to people like Fletcher or Spruance or anyone.* He may have told Spruance, because he could probably trust him. But I would say that Nimitz was to be certainly commended, although that's perhaps a little bit impertinent. But Nimitz appreciated the necessity for security that a lot of other people didn't. And Nimitz's answer to that problem was he didn't tell anybody where he got this information and it was not necessary.

Q: But I wondered where the daily traffic came from to the Lexington.

---

*Rear Admiral Raymond A. Spruance, USN, commander of a carrier task force at Midway, subordinate to Fletcher.

Rochefort - 184

Captain Rochefort: Oh, it came from Nimitz. It would never come from us.

Q: No, not from you, but Nimitz would say to Layton send Fletcher a message saying so and so.

Captain Rochefort: Yes.

Q: And you were getting daily reports from the Japanese fleet and where they were and telling Nimitz.

Captain Rochefort: No, we weren't. All we had was their operation order, you see. We had an operation order for the Japanese commanders and which we managed to more or less completely read this operation order, translate it. Decipher it and translate it, more or less completely. There were some blank spots in this thing, of course, which we filled in and which turned out to be correct. These I gave by radio to Nimitz. Actually it never went by radio. This would be hand-carried over to Nimitz. And we would go on the air to CominCh. This was all. There were the two addresses, and they were the only two people who could read it, because Stroop on the Lexington was not capable of reading our traffic.

Q: Oh no, there was no implication of that, and I didn't

ask him, because I wanted to ask you instead.

Captain Rochefort: We did not send our traffic to anybody except to CinCPac, and later CinCPOA* and CominCh. Now later we established a channel with ComSoPac,** who would be Admiral Halsey, and then later after that, then this went generally to the Third Fleet and the Fifth Fleet which would be Halsey and Spruance. We later expanded it. This, of course, at the direction of Admiral Nimitz. But the idea there was that it goes through somebody like, say, Admiral Nimitz. He confuses the whole issue by just saying I have reliable information to the effect, but he never discloses the source of this information, which is imperative.

Q: Lord makes the comment that he told Layton, "Now look, I don't know anything about this intelligence--communication intelligence--so it's your job to act like you are Yamamoto and act accordingly in your advice to me."

Captain Rochefort: That's right. Now Admiral Nimitz may have gotten this idea from me, because he visited our place shortly after he took over command.

Q: He did come to see you.

---

*Commander in Chief Pacific Ocean Area.
**Commander South Pacific Area.

Rochefort - 186

Captain Rochefort: He came over to see us as a sort of a little inspection. This was, I would say, in December of 1941. He came over and made us a little inspection, and this was probably completely unsatisfactory from his point of view, because at that time I only had one object, which was to read the Japanese traffic.

Q: Did he take lots of time for you to explain how you did all this?

Captain Rochefort: No, I never even bothered about this. I may have even been a little bit abrupt with him or possibly from his point of view unsatisfactory in that I wasn't paying too much attention to what he was saying to me or things like that. I couldn't recall any of that stuff at all, because I was interested at that stage of the game in what was in this message. That's all I'm interested in. I don't care about any commander in chief or anybody else.

Q: Strange that he would come to see you, however, when you were still Com 14.

Captain Rochefort: Well, I shouldn't say that he came to see me. What he was probably doing that day was making an inspection of Com 14, probably. Maybe the admiral then, who I think was still Admiral Bloch, maybe he brought him

Rochefort - 187

down to see me.* This may have been. I don't recall but I do remember he was over there shortly after he took command. I would probably just be informed by Admiral Bloch that I be prepared to receive commander in chief about 11:00 o'clock or something like this.

Q: Which was the usual inspection for people taking over a job. But not to come in and find out what you were doing.

Captain Rochefort: No. But it may be that at that time I gave Admiral Nimitz the germ of the idea of what he was supposed to have told Layton later on, about the task of these people which was to the general effect that my job involved telling my immediate superior what the Japanese are going to do tomorrow. That's my job. I don't tell them the day after it happened. They already know this. As a matter of fact, I kept drumming that into our people there that your job is to tell commander in chief today what the Japanese are going to do tomorrow and not yesterday. If you can't do this, then you've failed. It's my opinion that that really is the function of an intelligence officer.

Q: Yes, you had said that and made it, I thought, very clear.

---
*Rear Admiral Claude C. Bloch, USN, who had been Commander in Chief U.S. Fleet in the 1930s, was Commandant 14th Naval District in December 1941.

Captain Rochefort: There's no point at all in telling your immediate superior what happened yesterday. He already knows this. But you tell him what's going to happen tomorrow, what the enemy is going to do tomorrow. And I may have told Admiral Nimitz at that time the thing that I used to tell our people very often. Your job here is as a member of the Japanese Navy general staff. You are developing plans. You put yourself in the place of the Japanese Navy commander. What is he doing? To do this, you do not need to know what we're doing, you don't need to know anything about our own. As a matter of fact, it's better if you don't. And for that reason, I never paid any attention to what we were doing. I didn't know; I didn't want to know. Because if I knew, then this would tend to let me copper my bets. I would say this was probable, on the other hand, or something like this.

Q: It would influence or probably affect your thinking.

Captain Rochefort: Yes. So I gave him my opinion as to what was going to happen, based on Japanese Navy traffic.

Q: And you didn't wait to be asked, what do you think in these evaluations. You did them what, daily? You said the summary.

Rochefort - 189

Captain Rochefort: Yes, the summary would always be daily. This we were doing in peacetime. This we would do prior to December 7.

Q: And your forecasts--how often would you do that? On your own, daily, weekly, or whenever you had anything to say?

Captain Rochefort: In a case of, say, Coral Sea or Midway or in the case of some specific operation, then we would concentrate our men and everything would be related to that operation. We would start in, generally, by saying that certain units of the Japanese fleet are integrating into each other and there's been a change of command. We notice that CarDiv 3 that used to be working with the submarines has now been detached and is now working with ComCarDiv or something like this, you see, and this would gradually develop into a picture. Then, depending on their movements, you might find, for example, in the case again of Coral Sea, you might find that the carriers who had been dealing with, talking with Kure were now talking with Truk or maybe Rabaul.* Well, what's the purpose of this? Well, the purpose obviously is that they have some dealings with Truk or Rabaul, and this can only be for future operations and they are moving down to that area or through that area.

---

*Kure, Truk and Rabaul were the sites of Japanese naval bases.

Rochefort - 190

Q: They're going to do something with it for sure.

Captain Rochefort: They're going to do something with that. They are not interested in Ominate or other bases; they are interested in somebody else. So obviously, then, they are going to be connected in some way or another with Rabaul or Truk. This is common sense actually. It's not real intelligence; it's common sense. We would develop up from that then, and when you get to the actual operation itself, then, of course, the best thing to have is a copy of the operation order on which the ships are operating. This is common sense, too.

Q: Yes, but that would be very nice but certainly unusual.

Captain Rochefort: Yes, you don't normally get this. You get this very, very seldom. We had this in Coral Sea.

Q: And again at Midway, didn't you?

Captain Rochefort: And again at Midway, we had this with an additional advantage, that at Midway we were able to, based on this incomplete information and hints, little changes of plan, changes of location--you could give some advanced warning actually is what it amounts to, advanced warning that there is something developing in this particular area, you see, and this way would be to alert them, our own people. We didn't know why; they may be just congregating in a certain area because of some operation of ours which I wasn't even cognizant of.

Q: But that's for the evaluation then of Layton.

Captain Rochefort: I'm supposed to be, which I used to try to urge these people to remember, I'm the Japanese General Staff. This is what I'm going to do, and I'm not at all interested in what our own people are doing. I'm not interested in this at all.

Q: I think you give an awfully good picture really of what your operation was.

Captain Rochefort: It's difficult to explain to somebody that's not experienced or hasn't had the knowledge of, say for example, fleet operations. So many things become involved that actually it is really logic, is all it amounts to--it's just logic.

Q: Logic to you but not necessarily logic to other people.

Captain Rochefort: Well, possibly not.

Q: Because, for example, you said that when you gave these evaluations, I'm sure more often than not, there was somebody who wanted to say, "How do you know? You sit down in that little basement, and what do you know about the Japanese?"

Captain Rochefort: For example, I think possibly the greatest area of disagreement between the Army and even CominCh, our own Navy, and my office and certainly Admiral Nimitz's office was what was the target of these Japanese units, assuming that those Japanese units are involved in some operation. What makes you think that the target is Midway? Why wouldn't this target more properly be Seattle or San Francisco or something like this?

Q: San Diego.

Captain Rochefort: San Diego or Pearl Harbor. For a very simple reason, the Japanese didn't have the ships.

Q: The transports?

Captain Rochefort: They didn't have the transports.

Q: They had the fighting ships, didn't they?

Captain Rochefort: They don't have the tankers, they don't

Rochefort - 193

have the transports, they don't have the refrigeration ships, they don't have the supply line. This is why they can't go to San Francisco. Wouldn't it be ridiculous for the Japanese, say, at the time of Midway, wouldn't it be ridiculous for them to, say, go on to San Francisco for the purpose of bombing?

Q: It would have accomplished nothing.

Captain Rochefort: It would have accomplished nothing at all, no damage to speak of. They place themselves then 2,000 miles to the east of whatever the American Navy has got at Pearl Harbor, and we know that the American Navy at that time had three carriers in Pearl Harbor. Are the Japanese going to place themselves 2,000 miles to the east of these American units?

Q: Plus the fact that they would be subject to shore-based planes then.

Captain Rochefort: They'd be subject also to our shore-based planes off San Francisco in the area. Well, obviously this is stupid.

Q: You never underestimated them either, did you?

Rochefort - 194

Captain Rochefort: No.

Q: When you say that would have been stupid, you never underestimated them?

Captain Rochefort: No, this is one thing the Japanese aren't going to do. We wouldn't have done it, and I don't think the Japanese--well, anyway, in any event, they didn't have the shipping to do it. This is the very simple answer.

Q: Although they had the fighting ships, they didn't have the support ships.

Captain Rochefort: It takes a vast amount of supporting units. If you talk to any planning officer with any experience or any naval officer with any experience, and you tell him that you plan on doing this, he'd look at you in amazement, like you were out of your mind.

Q: Well, our whole drive across the Pacific is the first time it had ever been done by anyone anyway with the service squadrons and all of the support.

Captain Rochefort: It took a tremendous amount of support of backup units.

Rochefort - 195

Q: That really was our secret weapon, if you can use that phrase--besides you.

Captain Rochefort: Yes--no, I think this is our greatest area of disagreement. I cannot understand why CominCh--I never have been able to understand why CominCh gave any more than a couple of thoughts to the idea that this operation was to be directed against the mainland of the United States, because it was simply beyond the capability of the Japanese. It was beyond the capability of the Japanese, for example, to follow up on their Pearl Harbor attack. It was beyond their capabilities, and people were talking about the Japanese invading Pearl Harbor on December 7. This is sort of ridiculous, because they didn't have any ships. We could tell with a reasonable degree of accuracy what they had available and where these things were.

Q: And actually they did know something about the Japanese Navy and its capabilities even without your interpretation. It wasn't anything mystical.

Captain Rochefort: Oh no, there's nothing mystical about this thing.

Q: I mean that particular phase of it.

Captain Rochefort: The commanding chief, whoever he were, would certainly be far more experienced and far more capable than anyone else around with his knowledge and experience, and he was capable of making these estimates himself or judgments himself. But in the case of Midway, we knew that this was again going to be not an air attack on Midway but an attack and then an occupation of Midway, because the Japanese were bringing along such things as refrigeration vessels and about seven or eight transports with about 15,000, as I recall, Japanese troops. So you don't have these 15,000 Japanese troops coming along for an excursion to see an air attack or something. These people are there for a purpose. For what purpose? The purpose of occupying the islands. Then you further expect right after that then a buildup and a movement of Japanese planes from the Marshall Islands into Midway, after they had been captured and garrisoned. This would just generally follow. So that if you say that you are going to have carriers, which means an air attack, you might have surface ships, which might mean a bombardment or protection of the carriers, and this would signify an air attack. Now, if in the same outfit you find a movement of ships carrying personnel on transports, then this would give you reason to think about possibly an occupation. That was an amphibious operation and occupation. We had none of that on December 7th, so you can forget about that. We had none of that in Coral Sea other than small army groups being transported along the coast.

Q: There was an invasion force, however, in Coral Sea, wasn't there?

Captain Rochefort: There was a small outfit there to take care of the tip along Milne Bay and Port Moresby but not to the extent that we had had at Midway. You see, these were relatively small units. It was just the Japanese Army being transported from one side of New Guinea to the other. That's all that amounted to. And again in the case of Midway where you had an organization which consisted of a very powerful air group. Also lying 600 or 700 miles to the westward was the main Japanese force of battleships and a couple of small carriers and then coming from the Marshalls there was a group of ships being escorted by CruDiv Seven, which was the very powerful heavy cruiser division of the Japanese Navy, consisting of some 15 or 20 vessels. This was, of course, the occupation force. Therefore, then, this only left up north a small grouping of ships--a few carriers, small carriers, and a couple of cruisers, as I recall, and a small number of transports. This could best be described as just a diversionary force, which is what I think the Japanese called it at that time.

Q: I just wondered how you finally convinced Admiral Nimitz, because I'm sure there were a lot of people who brought to his attention the danger of taking your estimate 100%.

Captain Rochefort: Well, I would, of course, like to think that Admiral Nimitz was pretty intelligent himself. And, of course, then at that time we had some pretty capable people on the staff who would, of course, see all this and come to the same logical conclusion. It was only logic. I mean, there was no brainstorm involved in this thing at all; it was just a logical procedure.

Q: Wasn't there one incident that was fairly influential in their thinking about the use of AF as to what it meant.

Captain Rochefort: A lot of people have made much to do about that, and I honestly see no reason. Actually, we had hit on AF and, they also used the letter MI, I might say, on occasion. They used these things interchangeably. We came on that actually because we noticed that the first letter A used previously always referred to areas around Alaska and the Hawaiian Islands. For example, the attack on Pearl Harbor on December 7th was made on AH. Now AH can only be Pearl Harbor, because it was the only place where four or six Japanese carriers delivered a massive air attack on December 7th, 1941.

Q: So any time there was a reference to that, then you knew they were talking about Pearl Harbor.

Captain Rochefort: We knew this, and then gradually they began talking about an AG and an AF and other places. AO was somewhere up in Alaska as I recall. It naturally follows then that A followed by another letter was somewhere in this area, and we also noticed that when the Japanese made their second attack on Pearl Harbor, which was in February of '42, and this has very seldom even been mentioned, the planes took off from the Marshalls and refueled at A-something or other, which turned out to be French Frigate Shoals, because the Japanese had some submarines there and they flew the planes from the Marshalls to this A-something or other and they took off again and attacked Pearl, flew back and refueled again at the same place--French Frigate Shoal.

Interview No. 3 with Captain Joseph J. Rochefort, U.S. Navy(Retired)

Place: Captain Rochefort's home at 429 Via la Soledad, Redondo Beach, California

Date: 5 October 1969

Subject: Biography

Interviewer: Commander Etta-Belle Kitchen, U.S. Navy(Retired)

Q: You had just made reference at the end of the other tape to the use of the symbol AF and explaining that that was always related to the American theater. Can you start from there and go on?

Captain Rochefort: Well, generally--and this is somewhat repetitive, I suppose--when referring to geographical areas or geographical places, the Japanese developed a simple little code referring to cities, counties, states, countries, and areas by two or three Roman letters. Very quickly it became apparent that these, in the Pacific at least, where the letter A appeared, were invariably American. For example, on December 7th the Japanese reported they had made an attack on December 7 on the place which they identified as AH. Now obviously this has to be either the island of Oahu or some part of the island. It doesn't take any great amount of intelligence to determine that. It was the only place that they had attacked on December 7th by air and in which they had inflicted great damage and sank so many battleships and so much of this and so much of that. So obviously, then, AH becomes Oahu or Pearl Harbor or some part of Oahu. Similarly when during the battle of Midway when they were going to attack and occupy a place called AF, this obviously was also some American geographical spot or bay or city or area or something like that and the question arises as to what AF is.

Q: A always means American.

Captain Rochefort: A means some American position or land area or possibly some bay or harbor or something like. Just to digress for a moment, this was a very useful tool of the Japanese, because it assisted them in any of their references. For example, during the activity in and around Australia in early 1942 they were forced to spell out many places which had a very great assistance to any cryptanalyst. They had to spell out places like Alice Springs and places like that. And there were numerous others where they were forced to spell these out because apparently in this little geographical code or cipher they developed, they had not assigned any values to places such as Darwin and all that sort of thing and this, as I say, was a very great assistance. So it is a useful thing. Actually it's somewhat similar to--we developed a thing by calling them an operation, Operation This or Operation That--and it serves the purpose of reducing the number of times that you've got to identify some area by spelling it out. In any event, AF was obviously some place in the Pacific under American control. And in reference to that, that was apparently to be the target area. Also other places such as, AO, AOB, and all this sort of thing, were also targets but very minor. The selection of AF as meaning Midway by Station Hypo was made just as a result of a few logical steps. AF has to be in the Pacific; AF has to be under American control. It was a place which was in close proximity to the place that the Japanese used as a refueling for their reconnaissance or attack or something like this in February 1942, as I recall. This thing some people referred to as the second attack on Pearl Harbor.

Q: I'd love to have you enlarge on that.

Captain Rochefort: We will then as soon as we finish this thing. I've forgotten the terms that they use. This was possibly AG or something like that, and it had to be somewhere in the mid-Pacific, probably along the Hawaiian chain leading up to Midway.

Q: AG was.

Captain Rochefort: AG was obviously, because we determined from other information we received that the Japanese refueled their seaplanes and took off from the Marshalls and refueled at this AG place and then went on to deliver an attack on

Rochefort - 203

AH. Now, AH we know was Oahu or a part of Oahu. Therefore, AG had to be somewhere between the Marshalls where the planes took off from and the island of Oahu, and it was also within close proximity because, as I recall, the Japanese in their orders to the planes made mention of the fact that the Americans maintained a rather extensive air search from AF. So AF then had to have some airfield on it or seaplane bases and the only thing that we had was, of course, Midway. Therefore, by no exceptional stress of intelligence AF then would have to be Midway QED. And the amazing part of this whole thing is that many people could not accept this line of reason. There was no other line of reason, just none at all. Therefore, we were quite impatient at Station Hypo that people could not agree with our reasoning, because they had the same information that we had, and they should have without any particular stress on their brain come up with the same answers.

You asked a question a while back about this so-called second attack on Pearl. This, as I recall, was in February of '42 and by this time, of course, we were reading partially, and from this source we received indications that the Japanese were going to conduct what I would prefer to call a reconnaissance of the Pearl Harbor area for the purpose of determining what progress we had made in repairing ships in the harbor and so on. Their idea of doing this was to send several seaplanes, which were land based, from the Marshall Islands to Pearl, and in view of the distance involved they would have to be refueled. They proposed to do this by means of submarines to refuel at some spot en route somewhere along the Midway chain. It appeared that this would be done somewhere in the vicinity of French Frigate Shoals, which had refueling facilities. The Commander in Chief Pacific was informed of this, and it developed later on some additional detailed information was also available and furnished to Admiral Nimitz's organization as well as Com 14. The planes did depart Midway, did refuel at French Frigates...

Q: You mean "depart Marshalls."

Captain Rochefort: Marshalls, and did refuel somewhere in the vicinity of French Frigate, did approach the Hawaiian Islands and did circle the Islands and did actually drop a few bombs. One as I recall was in the vicinity of the Punch Bowl[*]--and departed, more or less unmolested.

Q: Now did you know they were coming ahead of time and you had told Nimitz ahead of time.

Captain Rochefort: We had told Nimitz and we had told Com 14 who was responsible for defense of Pearl Harbor. We had told them. I have no way of knowing whether they proceeded

---

[*]Punch Bowl--the crater of an extinct volcano near Honolulu, now a national cemetery.

Rochefort - 205

to act on this or whether they were not going to act. This was beyond my affairs. This was no affair of mine, except the next morning Com 14 sent for me and was quite irritated because these people had appeared and had flown more or less unmolested over the island of Oahu. It was actually incredible.

Q: It could have been the whole Japanese attack over again, based on that.

Captain Rochefort: It could have been. Of course, there was no way in which I could interfere.

Q: What did you tell him?

Captain Rochefort: I told him that this information had been furnished his office and had similarly been furnished to Commander in Chief Pacific somewhat in detail and in sufficient time for them to take any action which they wished to take. Apparently they decided to take no action. So Com 14 was apparently unaware of this information, and I never questioned, of course, what CinCPac decided to do. I was told later by informed people that the attack was made, as I say, more or less unmolested, because the Navy had no airplanes at that time capable of repelling this attack or destroying the incoming aircraft. The Army said that they only had one-place fighters, and who could expect a fighter pilot to not only fly the plane in darkness but also to approach and make an attack on any enemy plane. Therefore, nothing had been done about it, and no action was taken on this information.

Q: How did you react to that?

Captain Rochefort: I just threw up my hands and said it might be a good idea to remind everybody concerned that this nation was at war. That's all I could say. I mean, I can't say any more. We can give them the information, but if they don't wish to act on it for some reason or another, this was beyond my control and it was none of my business. But the Army air's approach to this question was completely incomprehensive to me that they could not use a multi-seat plane because it was too slow and they could not use a fighter because, while it did have the speed, these were all single-place and you couldn't expect them to do all these operations to fly and to shoot and particularly in darkness. Fortunately, as I say, no damage resulted. I think there were possibly two bombs dropped, although there was some vagueness on this also. We did not at that time, of course, develop such things as bomb recovery or have any search teams go out and find out whether these bombs were in fact Japanese or whatever they were. We had not developed that capability at all. It was just one of these things that you look on in amazement and wonder what happened.

Q: It's hardly a glorious incident, is it?

Captain Rochefort: It's not a very glorious incident. You won't find very many references to this anywhere along the line.*

Q: I can understand why, can't you? You said that nobody made much reference to it because they weren't very proud of this.

Captain Rochefort: Yes, of course, with the press of events or one thing and another we never followed this thing through as to why the incomplete action and it's not my responsibility. I was a little surprised at the lack of preparation.

Q: You must have been thoroughly frustrated and disgusted.

Captain Rochefort: To a degree, I would say, yes. Of course, my reasoning was that we had informed the authorities of this so-called reconnaissance or attack, if you will, and whether they took any action or not was their responsibility.

---

*The incident is described in Jasper Holmes' Double-Edged Secrets, pages 59-61 and in the U.S Naval Institute Proceedings, May 1953, pages 478-485, and August 1953, pages 897-899.

I naturally assumed that their reasons for not taking any action were very sound, and therefore it wasn't any of my business. This is difficult for people to understand, but it was barely possible that it was discussed in detail at CinCPac, and it was also barely possible that they decided it was to the best interests of everything and everybody that we ignore this.

Q: Is that possible? Do you really believe that?

Captain Rochefort: No, but you've got to stress this thing, because he was responsible and positive that he saw this information because I discussed it with the chief intelligence officer, Layton, and whether or not they took any action on it was their concern. Now maybe one explanation would be that Admiral Nimitz turned this information over to the Army air people and relied on them to take action. It is very possible. I don't know. As I keep repeating all the time, it was not my responsibility.

Q: Oh, I can understand that, but I can understand also that a natural reaction would be one of frustration.

Captain Rochefort: Yes, this is true. Well, anyway, I just mentioned it in passing. Did you have some other questions?

Q: Yes. First, we haven't mentioned--well, that ends that and you were getting on to Coral Sea by that time, and Midway. You haven't mentioned Captain McCormick who was the war plans officer.* Did you have any relationship with him at this time?

Captain Rochefort: I had known him. He, in the capacity of a rather senior officer and a very well respected officer, and me in the capacity of some perhaps impertinent lieutenant or lieutenant commander. I had known Captain McCormick, and I thoroughly respected his ability and I met with him after he became the war plans officer for Admiral Kimmel, I believe.

Q: I was of the impression that he was appointed by Nimitz to be the devil's advocate in relationship to the information which you provided.

Captain Rochefort: This is possible. I have no knowledge of that. As I keep saying...

Q: But I thought he worked directly with you.

Captain Rochefort: I probably discussed with--there were three or four officers, as I recall that during, say, the six or eight months subsequent to December 7th that would

---

*Captain Lynde D. McCormick, USN.

come over to my office. I don't recall going to CinCPac's headquarters except two or three times, so therefore they must have come over to my place, and we may very well have discussed it. I do not have any detailed memory on that part. I do recall Captain McMorris coming over on more than one occasion, usually late at night, and we'd have a cup of coffee together and discuss personalities and that sort of thing. But this was merely because, I think, because of the fact that I had the privilege of serving under Captain McMorris on several occasions before. Once I was his assistant on the Hawaiian detachment when he was the force operations office for Admiral Adolphus Andrews, and prior to that I think he was the navigator of the California when I was on there as a member of the staff of Commander in Chief, United States Fleet.

Q: Admiral Reeves?

Captain Rochefort: Admiral Reeves' staff. And I think for a period of time there Captain McMorris was the navigator of the California, and that was when I first met with him.

Q: The story goes that in order to convince officers that Midway was the aim of the Japanese that a message was sent relating to lack of fresh water on Midway. Is that...

Captain Rochefort: Yes, it is true. I recall such a message. The formulation of this or the idea of sending such a message has been attributed to me. It may or may not have been. It may have been Layton's idea. It may have been someone else's idea. In any event, this was not sent in order to convince ourselves. This was sent in order to convince people who did not believe that...

Q: Oh yes, that was my understanding.

Captain Rochefort: It was sent for their...

Q: Not for yourself because you...

Captain Rochefort: We were already finished with this business. It was sent to convince some of the people who, having had the same information that we had, had not arrived at the same conclusion that we had. As a way of getting rid of this problem, and stopping all this discussion about where was AF, somebody--as I say, possibly Layton or possibly somebody in my office, possibly me, I don't recall because it was not that important--but we did send such a message by cable telling Midway to send us in plain language the following thing relating to shortage of water.* And sure enough, within two or three days, in one of the Japanese

---

*Jasper Holmes takes credit for the idea in his book Double-Edged Secrets, page 90.

messages the statement was made that AF was short of water.

Q: That should have convinced the unbelievers.

Captain Rochefort: It should have, but it didn't.

Q: It still didn't?

Captain Rochefort: Oh no, it didn't. I think a lot of this thing, as I've indicated before, was that our organization was the best one in that the people who were presumably the best informed by virtue of experience, knowledge of the language, and a much closer study of the Japanese and things Japanese than other people. There was no way in which special knowledge could have been gotten or explained in the form of briefings or discussions or anything of this nature to the people that were going to act on it, namely, the commander in chief, and there was no connection in between us. So we had this ridiculous situation where some people are so fully informed, were so fully informed, but they had no knowledge whatever of the Japanese mentality or of the language or anything else, and yet they were making the decisions based on their own hunches or whatever it might have been. This, I think, in the future should be avoided, and some provision should be made for assuming these special intelligence people are competent or capable and experienced.

Q: Well, you had the additional advantage of having had the fleet experience, too, and you explained that, I thought, very clearly before, that you were not just a technician. You understood all phases of it which made--that's why you were probably the greatest value in the Pacific in this relationship.

Captain Rochefort: Well, this might be an exaggeration. But, in any event, the organization that was in effect--and this was probably a little bit unique also, because the fleet intelligence officer, who should be the person on the staff to inform the commander in chief--he happened to be a very close personal friend of mine.

Q: And also a Japanese expert.

Captain Rochefort: And also a Japanese language officer and also, as I say, being a close personal friend of mine. I could not bypass, or--as we used to say in the Navy--I couldn't "bulkhead" him by going direct either to Admiral Nimitz or somebody on Admiral Nimitz's staff such as Captain McMorris, Captain McCormick, or Admiral Delany and people like that. I just couldn't do this sort of thing to Eddie, and yet it would probably have been better if I had, for example, been sent for by Admiral Nimitz and questioned,

Rochefort - 214

queried, or cross-examined about some of the estimates or some of the statements, some of the judgments that I had previously sent in as to why we did this sort of thing, why we believed that.

Q: Didn't he send for you?

Captain Rochefort: Oh no.

Q: I thought at one time--now again I'm...

Captain Rochefort: Well, this was more or less after the die had been cast, particularly with reference to anything in Coral Sea or Midway. After Admiral Nimitz had reached his decision, then he would send for me. As I said before, this was shortly after Midway in which my opinion was asked as to what the results were at Midway and what the Japanese then would do. This was after the thing was over.

Q: From my reading, I understood that after May 25th the message came in?

Captain Rochefort: Then, that was the second occasion. That was before Midway, but this was still after Admiral Nimitz had reached his decision. He had made up his mind, he had bought what we had told him, very fortunately for

Rochefort - 215

this country. He had bought this, and he had acted on it all except in one case, which was his disposition of the American submarines. But no one could ever question him on his disposition, because this was sort of a preventative measure--just in case we were wrong, or in case we were unsuccessful.

Q: Can you tell me about that May 25th message before we go on?

Captain Rochefort: Yes, the May 25th message was the final translation of the Japanese operation order of May the 20th, as I recall, or thereabouts, which was the final operation order issued to all the Japanese commanders. Then on May the 25th we completely read this message including the two so-called interior ciphers or codes, one of which would be the geographical thing and the other would be the date, time, and hour which was separately enciphered inside, and this presented the big problem, because we could tell them what was going to happen. The only two things we lacked were where and when, and these were especially enciphered within the basic operation order by the Japanese in a separate little cipher system. Now, the where was easily solved. There was no problem there at all. This was the AF and the where and all that sort of thing, no problem here at all. The date, time, and hours--then when--we were unable to get this, because to our knowledge this had only been used three times--or maybe this was the third time it had been used. I think that's more correct. This was the third time it had been used and we, of course, had the other two instances available to us which we kept studying. But unfortunately one of them was garbled, so we had nothing in which to prove or disprove our assumptions as to June 4th or June 8th or June 10th or whether it was July the 19th. We had no way of knowing. But by concerted attack by everybody concerned we were finally able to restore or to rebuild the little system just based on these three particular little incidents and admittedly, it was rather shaky, but it was the best we could do under the circumstances because, as I say, we only had three indications of its use.

Q: And you did indicate June 3th, 4th.

Captain Rochefort: We did reproduce the table, the little cipher table of months and days and hours, and we did make our assumptions then that this had to be in June and that days A would be commencing, say, June 3 or whenever it was in Alaska, which was a diversion attack, June 4th and so on and so forth. Also included in this was the time of takeoff and the location of takeoff and the direction of approach.

Q: Of the planes?

Captain Rochefort: Of the planes. So, as an example, this May 25th dispatch of ours, which was the final dispatch bearing directly on the operation--the Japanese operation--contained such things as where the Japanese aircraft carriers would be when they launched their planes, degrees and distance from Midway, and the hour and the minutes. Then, of course, the rest of the dispatch would be the strength of the attack and the composition of the attack forces and so on. This was perhaps the major problem, and this was the dispatch we sent, as I recall, on May the 25th, and that was the morning that Admiral Nimitz had sent for me to arrive at a certain time at his headquarters and I was late. The reason I was late was that we were still working on the final aspects of this dispatch and when I saw that we were working on it, I mean that this would involve an agreement among the senior people at station Hypo and would probably have included Dyer, Wright, Finnegan, the translator, Huckins, the radio intelligence officer, and possibly Jack Williams, also radio intelligence officer, and this message that went out then was our consensus of what the dispatch meant and what the dispatch said and our reasons for it and like everything else in station Hypo, any major decision of this nature would be the result of, you might want to call it, the staff conference. We never did call it things like that. We just said that we all agree with this. When I say "we," I am always referring to the people who were most experienced and the most knowledgeable. It might or might not have included Jasper Holmes. I would doubt that, because he would not be familiar to that extent with the things Japanese.

Q: Yes, his expertise was the location of ships.

Captain Rochefort: Yes, that was his expertise.

Q: Tell me, then, you were a half-hour late and can you tell me more on that incident--I don't mean incident, I mean the meeting in his office.

Captain Rochefort: No, it's not very clear in my mind, because I would much prefer to be back in our place working on other things, and I was just merely there for the purpose of just answering any questions that were directed at me by Admiral Nimitz or someone else present.

Q: Who all was present?

Captain Rochefort: As I recall, there would be Admiral Nimitz and some members of his staff and I believe Army Air Forces representative was there. I believe either General

Richardson or his representative was there and some of our own commanders.*

Q: Layton, of course.

Captain Rochefort: I don't even recall if Layton was there. There were not very many questions at that time other than what do you think the Japanese are going to do or something of this nature. Of course, initially I apologized for being late and merely I would say here is a copy of the dispatch that was just sent to ComInCh and to Admiral Nimitz. This would explain everything. This is the operation order under which the Japanese are going to operate.

Q: Weren't they aghast?

Captain Rochefort: More or less. There might have been some questions arise in people's minds and probably these were well-deserved questions to be expected. "What makes you think that there is going to be [for example, let's say] four Japanese carriers launching the attack 125 miles, 315 degrees from Midway at 0700 local time on June 4th? Why not June 6th? Why not six carriers? Why not have the major attack against Alaska, which you also mention in here?"

---

*Lieutenant General Robert C. Richardson, USA, Commanding General, U.S. Army Forces, Central Pacific.

and questions of this nature. I would attempt to answer those questions honestly and to the best of my extent fairly. Of course, somebody who had been living this development over for about two months to the exclusion of everything else and maybe three months just completely living in this atmosphere, I could not understand why there should be any doubt in anybody's mind.

Q: You couldn't understand how they could be so un-understanding. Sure. And they were probably just as aghast at the temerity of saying here is a Japanese operation order--unbelievable to them.

Captain Rochefort: Yes, it would be something of this nature. Well, I think this has a big bearing too on the credibility of anything like this happening in the future or to a similar situation today. It is the credibility you would attach to the person developing this. If you happen to know him well or trust him or believe that he is capable, then, of course, this makes the thing much easier. If you went into a sort of hostile atmosphere which history would tell you many other things--for example, Admiral Canaris in Germany--he had somewhat the same problems.* I'm not comparing myself with Admiral Canaris. Now, I had at CinCPac three or four pretty good friends whom I had been with before.

---

*Admiral Wilhelm Canaris was head of the German Abwehr, the nation's military intelligence force from 1935 until midway through World War II, when the intelligence functions were taken over by the SS. He distrusted Adolf Hitler and was arrested in the wake of the unsuccessful 1944 assassination attempt against Hitler.

Q: What was the atmosphere? Was it hostile or friendly?

Captain Rochefort: The atmosphere was very impersonal. Admiral Nimitz had asked me a question, and I would look over there and I would see four stars. And I would answer this question to the very best of my ability. But at the same time, without being impertinent or nervous or anything of this nature. I would undoubtedly have been sure of my position, but again I want to stress that all I can do in a situation like this is to explain my position and hope that the admiral accepts it. If he doesn't accept it, I do not get mad at him. After all, he has the responsibility; along with this responsibility is this horrible thing of making a decision, which people not familiar with military operations never seem to understand. This is an awesome power to give somebody, but he makes a decision and if he guesses wrong...

Q: It stops right with him and...

Captain Rochefort: It stops right there, and no one else can take this away from him, and no one else can help him. They give him their advice, which I was attempting to do to the very best of my ability, and whether he would accept it or not was completely up to him.

Rochefort - 222

Q: When you were late, was he mad?

Captain Rochefort: Well, much has been said about this--that he greeted me with his icy blue stare or something or somewhat cold. I wouldn't even remember this. It wouldn't make any difference one way or another. I would be aware of the fact that I was 30 minutes late for an appointment with the commander in chief.

Q: And you told him why.

Captain Rochefort: And I told him why, and I would hope that he would accept this. Very fortunately, Admiral Nimitz being the type man he was, he accepted it. He would understand this.

Q: What did he look like when he would ask you these questions? What was the expression on his face?

Captain Rochefort: Some people might be afraid, some people might be frightened, some people might expect to have their careers ended in mid-stream, that is to say, but those would not be my feelings on the thing at all. I'd just merely tell it and I had been around; fortunately, I had served under half a dozen or eight or nine extremely capable naval officers, in my opinion, extremely capable. And they didn't frighten me.

Q: Well, what did he look like? What was the expression on his face when he would question you? Can you describe it?

Captain Rochefort: No, just somewhat cold.

Q: Would he frown, would he look intent, or...

Captain Rochefort: No, I think, as I recall it--I'm no expert on Admiral Nimitz. As I would recall, it would be rather coldly impersonal. I say, I don't remember at this time what he said, or what he did, or anything else, but he would act like, say, Admiral Standley or Admiral Reeves or other people that I had served with; he would probably be rather impersonal. He'd be very polite.

Q: Did he seem to be doubtful?

Captain Rochefort: No, not that I recall. No, he would accept my statements. But what his decisions were, I have no way of knowing. He might accept them. He might be listening merely out of courtesy.

Q: Did he give you that impression?

Captain Rochefort: No, as I say, it was more or less

impersonal. Just why do you make statements like this or why did you arrive at this conclusion or how did you form this judgment, what was the basis of forming this judgment or that judgment?

Q: Did he seem quite knowledgeable in his questions?

Captain Rochefort: Oh naturally. This was the commander in chief.

Q: I know, but I'm trying to get a description of that interview.

Captain Rochefort: I couldn't help you actually. Admiral Nimitz has sometimes been referred to as the great compromiser. I would prefer to say that he was able to get dissimilar groups to work together.

Q: Isn't it funny how you can say almost the same thing and one is complimentary and the other is critical? The latter you must have in life to do any kind of a job when you're the boss.

Captain Rochefort: Getting a little off the field, just from the few times that I spoke with Admiral Nimitz and had any dealings with Admiral Nimitz, I would gather that he was the one person in early 1942 that could have exercised command without the mailed fist over such diverse people as, say, the United States Army and Marines and the United States Air Corps. He could work with these people and with a certain amount of give and take; he would probably attain what he really started out to do without giving the appearance of giving an order. I used to be amazed. I think I had occasion to go into Honolulu maybe once during the six months between December 7 and Pearl. I had occasions to go in there, I think, once or twice.

Q: Between what dates?

Captain Rochefort: Between December 7 and Midway. And I was no end impressed, in and around Honolulu they had barbed wire barricades particularly around the dock area. They had sentries scattered all around and all of this business and the place was as dark as the inside of a derby hat. We got to Pearl Harbor, and there were floodlights all over the place. There were people working there on a 24-hour basis. You never saw this downtown. Well now, it was ridiculous downtown, for example, and in other parts of Oahu where every precaution was taken against sabotage by the Army who was operating in that particular area and everything would be dark as a dungeon and so on and so forth. We'd go out to Pearl Harbor and just the reverse held true.

Rochefort - 226

Now, Admiral Nimitz was in a position to direct the Army who were doing, among other things as I recall, a lot of dredging around the harbor and a lot of public works around the Honolulu Harbor area. Now most of this work was being done by foreigners and among the foreigners were quite a few Japanese and Chinese, which the Army apparently felt very strongly about, not being able to differentiate between the two of them. Out in Pearl Harbor we took the other attitude which was that we've got extreme damage out there. This has got to be repaired, so let's get on with it. Now this was the difference, and yet as far as I know Admiral Nimitz did not direct the Army to alter their plans downtown and their activities downtown to interfere with these activities, whereas someone else might. But not Admiral Nimitz. He would fix in his own mind that this is their responsibility. He is the overall commander; he wants to do things differently from them; this is fine.

Q: You started this by saying in the meeting he was--or someone said he was a compromiser. Were you thinking of a specific incident in the meeting?

Captain Rochefort: Not at this particular meeting, no. I don't know if I mentioned it before or not, but to me this little incident explains quite a bit about Admiral Nimitz and his relationship with other segments of the armed forces. As I recall--and I'll try to make this very simple--this, I think, was the meeting after Midway and the question arose as to the situation within the Japanese forces. What were they doing? Had they actually retired and given up the idea of occupying Midway and so on and so forth? As I recall, during the course of this thing, the suggestion was made by someone present to send out some additional planes to Midway as a precautionary measure. Admiral Nimitz spoke to the Army Air Corps man who told him he had X number of planes that were suitable for use around Midway. However, he was very reluctant to send these planes out there, because these were all the planes the Army had on Oahu. You take these planes off Oahu--they were B-17s, as I recall--if they take these planes off Oahu, this is all we've got on Oahu. The Navy had nothing. This would take everything the Army had, and Oahu would be completely defenseless. The admiral reminded him that within the next 30 minutes or an hour or something the Saratoga was coming in from San Diego with a load of planes as well as its own air group and he volunteered that if the Army Air Corps would send out all of their B-17s from Oahu for possible use in the Midway area, then he would turn over the operational control of the Saratoga planes during their entire period of stay in Pearl Harbor.

Q: To the Army Air Corps?

Captain Rochefort: He would transfer the operational control to the Army Air Corps, at which point the Army Air Corps brightened up and agreed to send these planes. Admiral Nimitz asked him to get the order under way then. I noticed at the time that the Navy air man, who I think was Admiral Bellinger--I thought he looked a little bit surprised at the moment, but he said nothing and the conversation went on.* They discussed other things. Then at some later period, perhaps 45 minutes or so later, the Army Air Corps man said, "By the way, Admiral, you say that the Saratoga is due in today at Pearl?"

And he said, "Yes, it should be in at any moment now."

The Air Corps man said, "How long may we expect the Saratoga to be here?"

The admiral said, "Long enough to fuel, and then she will proceed to sea and load up the planes again." But by this time the B-17s were on the way to Midway.

Q: That's a good story.

Captain Rochefort: This, I would suppose, indicates something about Admiral Nimitz. I never thought that he had a sense of humor.

Q: I was going to ask you how long the Saratoga was going

---

*Rear Admiral Patrick N. Bellinger, USN, Commander Patrol Wing Two.

Rochefort - 229

to be there. The guy didn't think of it fast enough, did he?

Captain Rochefort: No, probably four or five hours or something of this nature.

Q: That's a wonderful story.

Captain Rochefort: I noticed Admiral Bellinger was apparently somewhat perplexed at this whole turn of events. He knew when the Saratoga was coming in, and he knew when it was leaving.

Q: But, of course, he kept his mouth shut.

Captain Rochefort: Naturally he kept his mouth shut and said nothing. But the Air Corps man may have been General Tinker,[*] I don't recall who it was--but it suddenly dawned on him about the possibility of the Saratoga not being in port very long--just long enough to fuel and take on stores and that sort of thing. But I thought it was very amusing. I think it explains quite a bit about Admiral Nimitz.

Q: Yes, it does. I hope it gets into his biography, because

---
[*] Brigadier General Clarence L. Tinker, USAAF, Commander Hawaiian Air Forces.

I think it's very revealing as to his capabilities and how he went about achieving his goal.

Captain Rochefort: He achieved his goal this way. If you want to call this a compromiser, then I suppose you could.

Q: I think that's just being very true.

Captain Rochefort: But he got what he wanted. He satisfied the people that wished to build up Midway just in case as a precautionary measure. He also had air protection at Honolulu by virtue of the Saratoga's air group which, of course, would be flying in and landing on the fields. So we would have a degree of air protection there, and he was satisfying everybody. And still he got these extra planes down to Midway, which was apparently his main objective.

Q: Now we have two meetings that you had with Admiral Nimitz and have you covered most of the incidents that you can recall from the first meeting?

Captain Rochefort: Yes, I think so. I think in looking back on it, it was obvious when Nimitz sent for me on May the 25th that he had already decided his course of action. He had already decided as to what he was going to do with reference to this alleged attack and occupation of Midway.

He had already made up his own operation orders by this time and the matter was closed. This would be a sort of, I suppose you would call it, a final staff meeting so that everybody was thinking alike.

Q: Is it possible that, having made up his mind himself, he wanted these other officers to hear from you one of the reasons that was his basis for his decision? Did that occur to you?

Captain Rochefort: No. This may have been, or maybe he wanted it clearly understood possibly in his own mind and other people around there as to one of the bases for him making a decision that he had already made. This may possibly have been.

Q: I am sure it was an extremely dramatic situation, wasn't it?

Captain Rochefort: No, you'd never think so at the time. It was just a staff meeting.

Q: But for men who suddenly for the first time realized that the whole Japanese operation order had been decoded and that the admiral knew it, and here was the man who had done it. I am sure this had to be dramatic.

Captain Rochefort: I don't recall that impression having been given, because Admiral Nimitz certainly up to that period of time had never divulged the source of his information to anyone. Now whether we had any hand in that or not, I don't know. I'm sure that Layton with his knowledge of communications intelligence--I'm sure that he had reminded the admiral of the implications of anybody talking, and he would probably have referred to this on numerous occasions. For example, at a meeting of this nature, you would never have the supply officer or anybody like that, or the doctors. You would never have anybody that was not essential.

Q: You really had the people who needed to know.

Captain Rochefort: And only these people, and then Nimitz would never tell them anything. He would never get into a discussion, for example, of what this communications intelligence is. He would never get into any discussion of this at all. Based on Walter Lord's book, apparently some people in the fleet thought that this information was coming from Tokyo. I'm sure that the Admiral would never disabuse anybody of that idea.

Q: You mean by spies?

Captain Rochefort: Yes. This would be typically Nimitz,

Rochefort - 233

I think.

Q: Oh yes, that would be good to let them think that.

Captain Rochefort: Let people think this. This is fine. It doesn't hurt anybody. He would never disclose, I don't think, any indication as to the source of this information. He would merely say that information had reached him which, in his opinion, was sufficient to act upon or was reliable or something like this.

Q: And yet on this day in the meeting he did divulge...

Captain Rochefort: Oh no, no. He just asked me maybe a question as to what my judgment was on this or...

Q: Oh, he did not say to the people there...

Captain Rochefort: Oh no, he didn't go into any discussions of my activities. Oh no.

Q: Did he tell the people that I have this message which is the operation order?

Captain Rochefort: No, the only time he mentioned anything of this nature was on the meeting held after Midway which would be June 5th or 6th in which he introduced me--not introduced me but made the statement in the course of the meeting that in his opinion, or in his mind or in his judgment or something else, that this--I think he initially put it on a personal basis by saying "me."

Q: This officer.

Captain Rochefort: Yes, this officer deserves a major share of the credit for the recent victory at Midway. He made a statement to this effect.

Q: To all hands that were present?

Captain Rochefort: Yes. These people again were people that he could rely on not to say a word outside the room.

Q: How did that make you feel when he said that?

Captain Rochefort: Well, as I recall, my reply which would have been typical of me then and now--I was doing my duty and being paid for it and it was the least I could do and that any credit that he might think might accrue or any value that he might place upon our services was due to everybody in station Hypo and not to only one individual.

Q: I'm sure that would be your reaction.

Captain Rochefort: I muttered something to the effect that I was just merely doing what I was being paid to do.

Q: Weren't you pleased?

Captain Rochefort: Oh naturally I was pleased. But, you see, even at this point I felt, and many of my people also felt over in station Hypo, that this December 7th thing was to a very great extent our responsibility and we had failed. Because when I was sent over there, it was my responsibility and I took it as my job, my task, my assignment that I was to tell the commander in chief today what the Japanese were going to do tomorrow.

Q: And yet you had not had the assignment of the code in which they were doing their traffic.

Captain Rochefort: This is true. These would all be alibis, all excuses.

Q: But it's fact, is it not?

Captain Rochefort: It might be considered a fact. But still the major fact from this whole thing is that our group was given an assignment and we had failed, in my opinion. And therefore, to a degree, the responsibility for Pearl Harbor belongs to us.

Q: But I want to clarify this. I understood that it was Washington which was working on the Japanese military traffic.

Captain Rochefort: This is true--naval traffic. This is true. But at the same time, I was sent out to this office as the officer in charge of this unit whose duties were as follows: to solve all Japanese naval systems with particular responsibility for one ********************. To me, I accepted the responsibility for the entire Japanese naval operation.

Q: But you actually had not started working on the code in which...

Captain Rochefort: No, we had not because at that time the understanding was that Washington would do the basic work on this, being backed up by station Cast at Cavite.

Q: But it's your personality which makes you accept the responsibility. Probably mine would too.

Captain Rochefort: I honestly, not with any desire for drama or anything like this--in my mind, I and the people working for me had failed.

Q: Did anyone ever give you any implication of that?

Captain Rochefort: No, nobody at all. But this is my personal feeling. And I carried this feeling on up through Midway. Now, at Coral Sea, which was really a better job actually than Midway--we did a better job at Coral Sea. When I say "we," I mean primarily the unit that used to be at Cast or Cavite and it was then done in Bellconner run by a young officer named Fabian. They had done a fantastic job, and we had merely helped them. We had backed them up.

Q: On Coral Sea?

Captain Rochefort: On Coral Sea. But they had done the major part of the work and in my opinion they had done an excellent job. All we tried to do was to assist them in any way possible, because we had more researchers, we had more personnel, we had perhaps more experienced people--at least we had more talented people than he had, at least we thought so--and therefore all we were doing was helping him. At Midway, of course, the thing was reversed. The fact remains that there was never any credit given for the intelligence job at Coral Sea, by the senior people. Therefore,

---
*Lieutenant Rudolph J. Fabian, USN.

our only opportunity up to that point had been Midway. And we had done what I considered a very creditable job on the thing.

Q: To say the least.

Captain Rochefort: Some people might say it was good or fantastic or exceptional or something like that.

Q: I would take one of the latter adjectives.

Captain Rochefort: Well, it depends on what you consider your job. For example...

Q: But you know when you are doing a good job, of course.

Captain Rochefort: Yes, and we were content. We felt that we had earned our pay, because we felt that we had done the job. All of us would much preferred to have been somewhere else. We would have much preferred to be on ships, but this was the job to which we had been assigned and the job that we seemed to be best fitted for, so therefore we did the best we can. Besides a lot of these people on the ships that were getting killed were friends of ours. And this, of course, gave us some additional impetus. But I do think in all honesty we did probably an outstanding job insofar

Rochefort - 239

as the Battle of Midway was concerned. This doesn't detract at all from the fact that we failed at Pearl Harbor.

Q: I accept that statement but...

Captain Rochefort: Later on we failed in several instances. We had failed when we lost the Indianapolis. Somebody goofed up there and we lost the Indianapolis with quite a few people on board.*

Q: Was that down in the Solomons?

Captain Rochefort: No, this was pretty well toward the tail end of the war.

Q: I remember the Indianapolis and the enormous loss of life, but I can't put it into the schedule.

Captain Rochefort: Well, somebody goofed off on this.

Q: Wasn't that a long time before they even discovered that the ship had gone down?

Captain Rochefort: Yes.

---
*The heavy cruiser Indianapolis was torpedoed and sunk by a Japanese submarine between Guam and the Philippines on 30 July 1945.

Q: Were you still in Pearl then?

Captain Rochefort: Oh no, no.

Q: You had gone a long time before this.

Captain Rochefort: I was completely out of the organization, I was completely out of sight.

Q: You mean the organization goofed.

Captain Rochefort: The organization goofed somewhere along the line. You're not about to pin the rose for a thing like this onto commander in chief. You're not about to do this. Nor can you blame somebody like, say, CominCh or something. It's much easier to blame somebody pretty well down the line and that doesn't amount to very much, which was done. These I would call goofs. You might expect this to happen. You don't want it to happen, but it's going to happen. Several other times during the first Solomons operation in the fall of '42 and this would be; some of these probably before I left and some after I left in which we for various reasons did not get the facts in time or didn't act on them in time and the result would be again that we'd have some losses down around Guadalcanal. Now one of these would probably be at Savo Island. I don't recall the circumstances around that, but if we had been doing our job, we should have been able to tell Admiral Ghormley and Admiral Turner, who would not have accepted it anyway, but Admiral Ghormley might have.* We might have been able to tell them what the Japanese were doing in order for him to take some preventive action.** I don't recall whether there was an operations order issued on that or not. This may have been done right on the phone, you see, so I wouldn't know. If it had been done by written word orally establishing this operation then, of course, we were not to blame because it never went on the air. So it was none of our fault then. I don't know what the details were because we were so busy at that period of time. But I always considered it a failure every time that we were unable to inform either Admiral Ghormley or after him Admiral Halsey when he becamse ComSoPac. When we were unable to inform these officers about the Japanese intended actions, I always considered that a failure.

Q: I understand your thinking and I understand the statement.

---

*Vice Admiral Robert L. Ghormley, USN, was Commander South Pacific Force at the time of the U.S. invasion of Guadalcanal in August 1942. Rear Admiral Richmond Kelly Turner, USN, was Commander Amphibious Force South Pacific.

**In the early morning of 9 August 1942, Allied Forces off Guadalcanal were caught by surprise in the Battle of Savo Island. A Japanse surface force reached the area unmolested to sink four cruisers, three American and one Australian.

Captain Rochefort: If you're going to do your job, you are successful every time.

Q: You hope to be.

Captain Rochefort: You've got to be. If you're not successful every time, obviously it is a failure somewhere along the line. If this dealt with any Japanese naval operations, then we considered ourselves as being the ones that failed.

Q: Is it true that right after the May 25th message that the Japanese did change that code?

Captain Rochefort: Yes, the thing you might say is that the curtain went down with this operations order. The curtain went down with that, and we were not reading anything in ********** for a period of possibly a month or so. Then by the concerted action and luck, concerted action on the part of Bellconner and Hypo and the luck of the Japanese making communication errors, we were able to get back into this thing in time to be ready again by August 7th with the landings in Guadalcanal. We were able to get back in. But we did have a blank period in here.

Q: By the grace of God, you got into the operation order for Midway, and there was no critical action in the following months.

Rochefort - 243

Captain Rochefort: Research was developed which I was not familiar with, of course, having lost all interest in this after the fact. After the thing was gone, there wasn't any point in chewing over any kind of cold meat or anything. This doesn't get you anywhere. Apparently research and study has indicated that the Japanese proposed to change this code system on 1 April, but they weren't able to do so for administrative reasons, and then they set 1 May. And they were still unable to do it, because they just couldn't physically get these documents out among all the ships and one thing and another. So they had to postpone this change to 1 June. But I think actually the change was along about May 23, 24 or 25, somewhere through there.

Q: Actually just immediately after the operations order.

Captain Rochefort: Yes, I think they changed that before 1 June. This was supposed to have been the date that they changed it. A little research will, of course, indicate that it's not particularly important today.

Q: So you saw Admiral Nimitz the time he came to inspect your office, you saw him when he called you and questioned you concerning the translation of the operation order--decryption rather, is a better word, isn't it?--and then when he called you to this office after Midway. And was that the time when he commended you and then asked about the damage or the intentions of the Japanese at the same meeting, or was it separate?

Captain Rochefort: No, this was the same meeting and in my opinion, what were the results and secondly, where were the Japanese now, and what were they going to do?

Q: And you were accurate and able to answer him in all his queries?

Captain Rochefort: Oh yes, we were able to tell him. We were able to make much more accurate assessments of the Japanese damage by reason of the fact that we had the Japanese dispatches as to what their losses were, so if somebody would come along--for example, if a submarine commander would come along and say that he had put three torpedoes into the battleship $\underline{X}$ or something, we would be able to tell him, we're awfully sorry but those were all duds and just let it go at that. Now he might get a little irritated at this, but similiarly when the Air Force was very beligerent about the sinking of one of the ships of CruDiv Seven and insisted that they had sunk the ship--which I told them was not borne out by the facts, because we had information at that time that the ship was still afloat and was en route to Japan. He said, "I thought you'd say that." And at

Rochefort - 245

this point, he produced pictures. I said, "Well, in the first place, this is not a battleship, this is a submarine which is making a crash dive."

"That's what you say" and things like this, you see.

Q: Who was it you were talking to?

Captain Rochefort: Army Air Force. They were, of course, very sincere.

Q: And they dropped a lot of bombs.

Captain Rochefort: It just so happened that their photo intelligence was perhaps not as good as the Navy's. It so happened through no fault of their own, they had received some minimal--aproximately no training in flying over water or of identification of ships from 20,000 feet up. And they were not particularly trained in this, and at that point there was probably no reason to have training on this.

Q: There was a lot of conflict between who had done the damage at Midway anyway.

Captain Rochefort: Well, you always have this, I suppose. Our problem was to try to give them, without divulging the source, give these Air Force people or other people, including our own people--the criticism is not intended just for the Army or anybody else--but there is always a natural desire to build up your own performance of duty. This can be expected. Again it would have been a little bit helpful to us if there had possibly been better coordination between my organization and, let's say, some photo interpretation organization. Identification of ships or identification of photos or something. We had not developed this capability at this time, which is another weakness in the entire scheme of things. Later on, before long, I understand that this was improved upon, particularly when we established the JICPOA (Joint Intelligence Center Pacific Ocean Area). We established this thing in which all of the phases were put under one roof. This was improved upon. We didn't do that. We didn't have time to do it, and actually we didn't have the desire to do it.

Q: Joint Intelligence, what was it?

Captain Rochefort: Joint Intelligence Center, Pacific Ocean Area--called JICPOA. First it was called ICPOA--Intelligence Center, Pacific Ocean Area--and then later it was called the JICPOA by bringing in personnel from other services.

Q: Lord tells of an incident--that because of your traffic, the Japanese were supposed to reconnoiter again before Midway

Rochefort - 247

in Pearl and that because of the knowledge which you had given Admiral Nimitz's staff, there was a big seaplane on duty and so the Japanese planes could not refuel. The submarine could not come up to refuel the planes, and as a result they did not make the reconnaissance?

Captain Rochefort: Yes, that was again in the area of French Frigate Shoals. I read something about that.

Q: Is that correct?

Captain Rochefort: I don't recall any traffic bearing on that. It may have been something we had missed.

Q: I thought it was something that you had disclosed, or was it because they did it before when they made the February attack on Pearl, maybe you just forecast that they were going to do it again.

Captain Rochefort: It's possible.

Q: Because, you see, it's accredited to you.

Captain Rochefort: Well, it might have been propr to have given us the credit for it. I don't recall it, very frankly. Now, if a study were made of all of the dispatches at that time and if you go back and historically analyze them, it might show up. We may have told CinCPac that a thing like this was in the air, or it had been ordered, or they might expect it or something of this nature or it may have been due to the initiative of Admiral Nimitz's aviation officer, who I recall was Captain A.C. Davis, who was extremely competent, most capable.* He would be capable of coming up with this idea himself. I don't recall. You've got to remember that at this time we were only interested in one thing at Station Hypo. We were interested in who is going to come to Midway and when and what are they going to do. We were not interested in any side matters at all unless they just fall into your lap. For this reason we just concentrated on the Kido Butai, and these were the people we were interested in. We always kept it in our minds that you also have Commander in Chief of the Rengo Kantai, the Combined Fleet.

Q: That's a new name to me.

Captain Rochefort: Rengo Kantai. This is Admiral Yamamoto of the Rengo Kantai—Commander in Chief of the Combined Fleet. Now we knew where he was and what his purpose was, 600 or 700 miles to the rear of the big ships and the battleships. We knew this. We also knew that there were another group of ships coming up composed of say CruDiv Seven as the covering

---

*Captain Arthur C. Davis, USN.

force. These were the very best Japanese heavy cruisers--
the Kumano and the Mikuma, and there were two more of them.*
We knew that and we also knew that they had tankers, they
had transports, they had refrigerated ships, food ships
and all that sort which you would associate with an occupation
and a landing. We knew all this, but the simple theme in
all of this thing, as far as we were concerned--where is
the Kido Butai, which was four carriers plus the required
other ships, and what are they going to do and when?

Q: Kido Butai?

Captain Rochefort: Yes, Kido Butai, the first striking
force. We might call it a task force, you see, or something
of this nature. This was the focus of all of our attention.

Q: And if anything else came in, okay, but otherwise it
was extraneous.

Captain Rochefort: We'd accept it. Yes, it was completely
extraneous, because in our own mind, it had no relation
whatever to the United States Fleet operations. The immediate
threat that was exposed there was the four Japanese carriers.
Then it follows if you can beat off this air attack or attacks

---

*The other two ships of Cruiser Division Seven were
the Suzuya and Mogami.

or can destroy their planes or destroy their carriers, you've got them just about where you want them. This just necessarily follows--we did that. We destroyed the four carriers by a fluke, but we still destroyed the four carriers, and the Japanese had to call off the entire operation. It was that simple.

No, I wouldn't remember--if I knew--I wouldn't remember any of these little details of operations.

Q: Did Admiral Nimitz recommend you for a decoration?

Captain Rochefort: Yes.

Q: And?

Captain Rochefort: It was turned down.

Q: By whom?

Captain Rochefort: CominCh.[*]

Q: Do you know why?

Captain Rochefort: This would be a very sad and disappointing story, and I would not think that anything would be gained

---

[*] Admiral Ernest J. King, USN.

Rochefort - 251

by going into it now.

Q: It's part of your life, however.

Captain Rochefort: It's part of my life, but it doesn't affect anything else.

Q: Well, this is biographical, you see.

Captain Rochefort: Well, let's put it this way.

Q: Let me ask you again. What did Admiral Nimitz recommend you for?

Captain Rochefort: The Distinguished Service Medal. Let's put it this way. Actually Admiral Nimitz didn't initiate this. Com 14, who, again, was my immediate superior, recommended this, and Admiral Nimitz forwarded it very favorably. He made some very nice remarks, and I advised against it. I advised against doing anything like this, because it's going to make trouble. Why is it going to make trouble? Because if you do this, then you are admitting, and if CominCh approves it, he is admitting that the intelligence work at Midway was done by Station Hypo and not by Washington.

Q: Well, what's wrong with that?

Captain Rochefort: If you admit this, then you admit that the statements that have been made the last three or four months by Washington--Station Negat--are incorrect. They were presumably our bosses. They had apparently convinced Admiral King that they were responsible for the intelligence at Midway. They were responsible. Now, these people were composed in the main...

Q: And yet Admiral King had gone to you direct on one occasion.

Captain Rochefort: Yes, by last April or thereabouts--in March or April, yes. That's true. But he is admitting this. This is my stand during the summer of 1942 and during this time, you will also remember we were having trouble with Station Negat.

Q: No, I didn't know that.

Captain Rochefort: We were having trouble with them, because they were attempting to exercise control over us by what I termed the bullying tactics or brow-beating tactics, something to bring us into line with their thinking.

Q: But this is Safford in Washington?

Captain Rochefort: No, no. Safford by this time had been

eliminated. And the--what I referred to as the opportunists--

Q: The Redmans.

Captain Rochefort: The Redmen and people of this group. They saw a way to promotion and pay in this operation and future operations. There might be some way here of getting promotion and pay by taking credit.

Q: And prestige.

Captain Rochefort: And prestige, yes. And this resulted eventually in an out-and-out argument.

Q: Between yourselves?

Captain Rochefort: Between ourselves, of which there was only me. I divorced my people from this whole thing. If there was going to be any reaction to this thing, it would come back on me and it was suggested by somebody at that time, why don't I just tell Washington to go to hell? I said, "Well, I can't do this."

Q: Who suggested this to you?

Captain Rochefort: I don't recall. This could be anybody

Rochefort - 254

on the CinCPac staff. But anyway, I eventually prepared a dispatch which said in effect that what is history is history. What happened in Midway, happened in Midway. I'm not at all interested in anything like that now. We've got other problems such as future operations in the Pacific, which is getting our place on a businesslike basis and so on and so forth, and therefore I'm not going to discuss any longer with Washington or anybody else any matters whch I consider as not important.

Q: That's history.

Captain Rochefort: That's history. I'm not going to discuss this matter any longer with you.

Q: And you sent this to Redman?

Captain Rochefort: I sent this to Washington--everything we dealt with was CominCh, you see--the only people we dealt with officially; we dealt with CominCh.

Q: And you sent this to CominCh?

Captain Rochefort: I sent this in the CominCh, and furthermore I'm operating under the instructions of Admiral Nimitz, who fully subscribes to this. And I showed this to Layton.

Rochefort - 255

Layton said the admiral has seen this and he agrees with it, and he said send it. Which I did send.

Q: Do you have a copy of it?

Captain Rochefort: No, I wouldn't keep a copy of that. This was all more or less interior.

Q: Plain language?

Captain Rochefort: Oh no.

Q: All code?

Captain Rochefort: This would all be in our own system. The only people that would know about this thing would be people we talked with. I was assured before I sent it that this had the approval of Admiral Nimitz and what it really meant was that from this day on, I am working for CominCh and CinCPac, and I'm not working any longer for you clowns back in Washington.

Q: Redman?

Captain Rochefort: Well, any of these people involved.

Rochefort - 256

Q: People who had taken over from Safford?

Captain Rochefort: Yes, people who had wrested control from Safford. This is really what it meant. That from here on in, unless you people have got something concrete to offer, don't bother me.

Q: And did they? Did that stop it?

Captain Rochefort: The answer to this thing, of course, was to order me to Washington for temporary duty. That was the answer to that, real fast. First, I was placed in charge of this new operation called ICPOA. I was the officer in charge of that.

Q: In Washington?

Captain Rochefort: No, no. In Pearl Harbor. This whole operation which would get me away from communication intelligence.

Q: You were taken out of the intelligence then?

Captain Rochefort: Yes, and put in charge of this whole operation. I refused to accept that. I just flatly refused to have any part of it.

Rochefort - 257

Q: Can we get dates on this now, so we can get chronology?

Captain Rochefort: No, this is all more or less of a personal matter anyway.

Q: Well, I mean is it '42? October '42?

Captain Rochefort: I would say in the summer of '42.

Q: The summer of '42. June to October?

Captain Rochefort: Yes, including this promotion thing and the medals and so on and so forth.

Q: Did Admiral King just come back and say negative, not approved?

Captain Rochefort: No, no, he never said anything.

Q: Oh, just nothing ever happened.

Captain Rochefort: No, nothing ever happened. I did this with the knowledge--I was told, with the knowledge of Admiral Nimitz, and with his approval. Then I was ordered back to Washington for ten days' rest and recreation, to have a little rest. I went back to work and said, "I'm not tired."

So, anyway, I had to go back to Washington, and I told everybody, "When I leave Pearl, I'm not coming back." I knew this. "I know I'm not coming back."

"Oh, yes you are, too." I was talking to Com 14, Admiral Bagley, and he said, "Don't forget, now, you come back. I was just talking to Admiral Nimitz and he wants you back here."*

I said, "Well, I'll tell you one thing. I'll bet I'm not coming back."

He said, "Well, you've got to come back, because Admiral Nimitz says so."

I said, "Well, then Admiral Nimitz had better straighten this out with Admiral King. But I'm predicting right now that I won't be back." Which was true. So I went back to Washington, and I was told that I was not going back to Pearl.

Q: Who told you?

Captain Rochefort: CominCh's people. I was not going to go back to Pearl, at which time I made several mistakes in a great big hurry, one of which just compounded the other. And the net effect was I was supposed to go back for some special work back around Washington, and I flatly refused. I was just not well, I think. I think that was the problem,

---

*Rear Admiral David W. Bagley, USN.

that I was not well and I was not thinking well.

Q: You had become overtired?

Captain Rochefort: Overtired. I was exhausted. But I still was well enough to have kept the job in Pearl. But unless I go back there as the officer in charge, then I'm not going to perform the duty in Washington. And this you don't do.

Q: It doesn't sound like you up to now.

Captain Rochefort: Oh, no, no. You just don't do these things. I said, "I'm not going to work for you guys. I'll tell you that right now."

"Oh, yes, you are, too."

I said, "Well, I've got news for you. No, Sir."

Q: Now this is between Admiral King's staff and Redman's staff or...

Captain Rochefort: Well, the whole outfit. This would be a combination of communications, Director of Naval Communications people and some members of Admiral King's staff. I did discuss the matter with several old friends of mine, including Admiral Reeves and several other rather senior officers, and they volunteered to assist me, but I told them I didn't need any assistance. So matters came to a point where I could go to sea. They said, "Well, what do you want to do?"

"I want to go to sea, preferably in a combatant ship. That's what I've been trained to do, and that's what I want to do. I do not want any shore job. I do not want to become involved in any non-combat activities."

Q: You would have liked going back to Pearl though, wouldn't you?

Captain Rochefort: I would have taken that, yes.

Q: As the officer in charge of the unit.

Captain Rochefort: Oh yes, I would have done that, but I would have only done it on my terms which was I was completely independent.

Q: And which you went there in the first place.

Captain Rochefort: And which I went there in the first place. Now this was completely unacceptable, and I could understand this. In Washington to have some people in the field engaged in this rather important communications intelligence job who would not submit to some of the control by Washington. I can see that this would be acceptable to them--but then I couldn't see. In any event...

Q: Did you take any rest at that time?

Captain Rochefort: No. In any event, I was told then that I couldn't go to sea unless I got cleared by CominCh. CominCh had a policy in effect which was very sound, and that was that people used in this type of activity were not to be allowed in the so-called war zone. This was very sound. We had already lost one very good officer. The commanding officer of a submarine chose to go down with the ship rather than be captured, because he had knowledge of future operations, so he just chose to go down with the ship, which is rather silly. Anyway, I was told I could go to sea, but I had to have a clearance from CominCh. So I got that clearance by calling everybody I could think of and in order to get rid of me then they said, "Okay, we're turned loose of you." Then I did get the offer of a job from the Bureau of Personnel through friends again--a very desirable job, as a matter of fact--and the promise of something in the future if I carried out this one assignment. But I had promised my wife who had come East with me and was then in New York--I promised her on Sunday, which was two or three days away, that we'd go up and see our son who was a plebe at West

Point. I told them I couldn't leave Washington then until after that. But this job had to be filled right now. As a matter of fact, the ship was sailing that day from San Francisco, and I could have had command of it if I hadn't been bull-headed, which was a very stupid thing for me to have done. So that was the story on that. But this was all personal and could have been avoided. It could have been avoided actually by Admiral Nimitz later on, by expressing himself forcefully to Admiral King. But again, this is Admiral Nimitz.

Q: He could have expressed himself while you were in Washington?

Captain Rochefort: Yes.

Q: How long were you around Washington?

Captain Rochefort: A week, I suppose, or something like that.

Q: I wonder if he knew what was going on.

Captain Rochefort: He was informed. I made all this information available to him, and I was assured that he had seen it--Admiral Nimitz had seen this information and had chosen not to act on it.

Q: One wouldn't know the reasons for it.

Captain Rochefort: No, this was maybe to gain some other end that he wanted. Maybe he was going to be gaining something else, maybe he didn't. But in any event, I did not go back to Pearl, so this takes care of Pearl Harbor.

Q: But then you did go to a job in October of '42 which was a real switch with Commander Western Sea Frontier. What did you do there?

Captain Rochefort: I was told by Western Sea Frontier that he wanted a Joint Intelligence Center set up combining Com 13--13th Naval District, 12th Naval District and 11th Naval District--and he wanted me to set up this joint intelligence center, which I did. This was actually in the Federal Building in San Francisco. That was before I wound up.

Q: Anything remarkable, any stories or anecdotes about that?

Captain Rochefort: It was a lot of fun.

Q: You enjoyed that. Of course, Mrs. Rochefort was with you, I'm sure. So that was pleasant to have that situation.

Captain Rochefort: Oh yes, she was with me then, and that was very pleasant. At least I knew generally what was going on, because we would get copies of quite a few dispatches and I could piece these things together and see what was in the wind and what was developing and so on and so forth.

Q: After Midway, you were in Pearl Harbor from, say, June until September, October.

Captain Rochefort: Oh, September, October--I've forgotten what that was. I think October--I'm not too sure.

Q: You went to Commander Western Sea Frontier in October '42.

Captain Rochefort: Well, that could still have been.

Q: If you were in Washington only a week, why you still could have left there. Were there any things happening during that time, do you recall?

Captain Rochefort: No, that was sort of a hiatus, sort of an interval in between.

Q: And you said that the beginning of the Solomons had taken place.

Rochefort - 265

Captain Rochefort: Yes, I was in Pearl then at that time.

Q: And that was when you said that you felt that there was a lack of success with that?

Captain Rochefort: Well, we felt that unless we had informed first Admiral Ghormley--and later on he was relieved by Admiral Halsey--unless we could inform him in time to make the proper disposition of his forces as a result of reported Japanese orders or actions and intentions, that we had failed.

Q: After Midway, weren't all of the members of your staff completely exhausted?

Captain Rochefort: Yes.

Q: Was there any opportunity to take a respite from the crushing hours and the schedules that you had set up?

Captain Rochefort: Yes, for some reason or another--I don't know who originated this--but for some reason or another, say two or three days after Midway when we were sure that everything was taken care of--after this thing, then I ordered all these people home and told them I didn't want to see them for three or four days. Their answer to this thing was to set up a party--I don't know where this thing was--

but somewhere on Diamond Head, and they got me up to this thing and this thing was a great big drunken brawl. That's all it was.

Q: Probably good for everybody.

Captain Rochefort: Good for everybody. So I remember there must have been 20 or 30 people around, and this was just a straight out-and-out drunken brawl. It was in a house--it wasn't in a hotel--we had sense enough to stay away from a hotel. Then after about two days of this, then we gradually drifted back and started off again.

Q: With the same terrible schedule?

Captain Rochefort: The same schedule, yes.

Q: 22 hours a day, 20 hours a day?

Captain Rochefort: Just about. Because by this time we had this new edition [of the Japanese code] we had to start reading as of yesterday hopefully.

Rochefort - 267

Interview No. 4 with Captain Joseph J. Rochefort, U.S. Navy(Retired)

Place: Captain Rochefort's home at 429 Via la Soledad, Redondo Beach, California

Date: 6 December 1969

Subject: Biography

Interviewer: Commander Etta-Belle Kitchen, U.S. Navy(Retired)

Q: We are going to continue on, Captain, with your activities. After you went out to the Western Sea Frontier and had the job there, do you want to comment on any of the duties that you had or any interesting items during that period of time?

Captain Rochefort: Well, at this time, you will recall, it was about the end of 1942 or the beginning of '43, and Commander Western Sea Frontier was very desirous of developing an intelligence center for the three naval districts under Commander Western Sea Frontier and asked me--or rather directed me--to perform such a task. I'm very much afraid that I really didn't have my heart in this, because about early '43 there was no question about the development of the war in the Pacific, and I would have been amazed had we had any Japanese activity anywhere to the east of Midway at this time. The Japanese were on the defensive, and I would anticipate no need actually for a really effective intelligence--joint intelligence organization--on the continental United States. I remained on that duty for a short period of time, and then I was ordered to command the ABSD 2, which was the second of the large floating dry docks, with the understanding that I would not take this ship to sea, merely to supervise its construction. This was a very interesting duty, but in the midst of it, if I remember correctly, Admiral Hart appeared in San Francisco in connection with one of the various inquiries at that time dealing with Pearl Harbor and asked me what my duties were, and I told him.* He made no comment when I urgently requested that he not interfere but just leave me where I was performing duties on the West Coast not involving intelligence. But almost immediately after his departure I was ordered back to Washington and eventually was put in charge of an organization which we called Pacific Strategic Intelligence Group for the purpose of providing information regarding future operations of the fleet--future planning for operations of the fleet. I performed these duties until approximately mid-August when the Japanese surrendered, at which point I was permitted to go to sea. I was given command of an APA** which I never did take command of this by reason of the fact that at that time they ordered the seventh inquiry into Pearl Harbor. This was a so-called senatorial inquiry, and as far west as I got was San Francisco--at which point I was ordered

---

*Admiral Thomas C. Hart, USN (Ret.), who had been Commander in Chief Asiatic Fleet when the war broke out in 1941.

**APA--attack transport, an amphibious warfare ship which carried troops and landing craft to an invasion beachhead.

Rochefort - 269

back to Washington and not permitted to leave the Washington area pending the pleasure of the Congressional inquiry.

Q: Tell me about that.

Captain Rochefort: Well, that was, as I recall, the seventh inquiry including the so-called Roberts thing, which was a travesty of justice actually. But, anyway, this was to be conducted by a joint committee of senators and congressmen to make a final determination of the responsibility, the blame and so forth.

Q: And the war is all over by now.

Captain Rochefort: Well, this was now in the end of '45 and the early part of '46, and if I remember correctly, I just remained in Washington until rather late, possibly February or March of '46. I was called as a witness. But this was not particularly important testimony, as I recall. It was just a repetition of everything that had gone on before.

Q: What did they want to find out from you?

Captain Rochefort: They wanted to find out--well, basically they wanted to find out why Station Hypo didn't do certain things, such as, providing the commander in chief with advance information and so on. Or why we weren't functioning as well as might have been expected, and apparently we answered the questions satisfactorily--at least I didn't go to jail. So that took care of that. Then eventually I couldn't go back to my ship, because by this time the command had been given to somebody else. And eventually then I requested retirement. I was sent to Terminal Island at Long Beach.

Q: Before you leave that, when we were talking before, you made a comment that while you were in CNO from April '44 to September '46 which is two years and five months--when you were in this Pacific Strategic Intelligence that you had said that you had a big bet here that you are missing because of the sources of information that you have and you're not using it for future plans.

Captain Rochefort: Yes, I made such comments.

Q: So didn't they say, well, you go ahead and do it then? Something of that nature?

Captain Rochefort: Yes, this was the--of course, when I first went back to Washington from the command of the ABSD-2, which as I recall, would be in April '44 or something like that--it was a perfectly innocuous remark on my part and should have been considered by the people in Washington that were responsible for preparing future operations, that were doing the advance planning for future operations, such as Operation Olympic. I merely pointed out that, which to me was merely an obvious conclusion which was it would be helpful to these planners if they had some indication or some estimate based on fact or logic regarding the Japanese capabilities, say, at the time that Operation Olympic was being planned for--six months or nine months in advance.

Q: This was the invasion of Japan?

Captain Rochefort: Yes, for that and the alternate scheme which, of course, would be Taiwan or Formosa. Any of these future plans which would enter the consideration should have this type of information available, provided the information was reasonably sound and it was not just some wild person's guess. I discussed the various sources of this information, the result being that I was ordered to organize a group which we named PSIS and which then produced several estimates regarding the Japanese capabilities, oh say, six months, nine months in advance.*

Q: Of course, which they should have used had it not been for the atomic bomb.

Captain Rochefort: Yes, which were then being planned.

---

*PSIS-Pacific Strategic Intelligence Section.

There were several operations being considered--one of which involved the next step being, as I recall, to go to Taiwan. Another one involved landing at Kyushu. It was my opinion that a unit, rather small unit, if they were competent and had the required source of materials, such as captured documents and all the messages going back to, say, 1941 or '42, could have, if organized properly--could have been of some value to the planners at the Joint Chiefs of Staff level. And as a result, we formed this PSIS, and in my opinion, it justified and actually provided some very good information. I have no way of knowing if this information was used or not, but this would involve of course all nameplate data and the numbers of ships being built or constructed or sunk and an analysis of the sinkings.

Q: What their capabilities would be?

Captain Rochefort: And then from this, then, we developed an estimate regarding Japanese capability regarding both personnel and materiel at any given point in the future.

Q: Did you ever have an opportunity to know how accurate your estimates were at the time the war ended?

Captain Rochefort: Yes, I asked several people that proceeded to Japan immediately upon the surrender, particularly the

USSBS people.*

Q: What's that mean?

Captain Rochefort: USSBS, the bombing survey actually, which was in the vernacular at that time, "who were you going to give credit for the victory in the Pacific." This was basically the idea. The team was sent out, as you probably recall, and arrived at Japan shortly after the surrender--immediately after the surrender--and then proceeded to various places, including Hiroshima, Nagasaki, and Tokyo, and any of the devastated areas which had been bombed by the B-29s--to attempt to make a survey regarding the relative effect of the attacks on Japan including those by the B-29s and including those by the carriers and including the A-bombs on Hiroshima and, of course, Nagasaki. Upon their return, I was told that our estimates were remarkably accurate, estimates that were predicated on either the forthcoming operations including Kyushu and Taiwan--our estimates were within 5% accuracy.

Q: Isn't that remarkable?

Captain Rochefort: This was done without too much of an effort on my part actually. We didn't really bear down on this to the extent that we had, say, in Pearl.

---
*United States Strategic Bombing Survey

Q: It was child's play for you, I presume, compared to what you had been doing before.

Captain Rochefort: Yes, it was relatively simple, because I could deal out most of these tasks to the very competent language officers and a large number of WAVE officers and WAVE enlisted people that I had. If I remember correctly, we had about 300 personnel attached.

Q: Is this PSIS?

Captain Rochefort: Yes.

Q: Did you? That's a large organization.

Captain Rochefort: It's much larger than I would have preferred, but of course what we did among other things in this PSIS, we reconstructed all the Japanese codes which we didn't have time to do previously. We reconstructed all of these, we developed a whole complete communications file, so we were prepared to state where all Japanese submarines were at all times during the war. Just minor little things. These were all very minor, and we made a couple of special studies.

Q: Were you used at that time?

Captain Rochefort: No, these would be more or less for reference purposes, basically. But they would furnish anybody that was interested, for example, say, the history of Japanese submarines during World War II. They would be very valuable there. They would also be very valuable in clearing up any questions such as how many submarines were off Pearl Harbor on December 7th? Because we had the whole communications file of Commander Sixth Fleet, commander of the submarines for the Japanese fleet. We had his whole communications file available for reference. This, of course, would be the true picture and even be much more reliable than what information we had back in '42 or '41.

Q: Did you determine any information which was different than you had known about before you came into the organization?

Captain Rochefort: Yes, it clarified a lot of points. For example, if we had reports of a Japanese submarine being sunk by somebody in the vicinity of Oahu, for example, on December 7th or the 8th or the 9th or the 10th, the reference material which we would prepare as a result of obtaining this captured material from the Marshalls would have cleared this up for anyone interested in making an actual study of it. These were all part of the material that was needed by the Strategic Intelligence Group in order to make their estimates, say, for 1945 or 1946, because they would be basic to the reference material that would be needed. This was not as desirable an operation as could have been made of it if we had really devoted our entire efforts to this sort of thing. But here again the war...

Q: Wouldn't it have been valuable if it had been started earlier?

Captain Rochefort: It would have been invaluable had it started earlier. In other words, I am trying to say that in any intelligence organization such as radio intelligence, your first problem, of course, is to find out today what they are doing tomorrow. You are not interested in the niceties of this or in the complete accuracy of it or the fineness of this deal. Now immediately upon the completion of this thing, then we could have what might be called the clean-up group, which is going to refine all this information, but you are not acting under a tactical situation, acting under sort of a strategic situation. But it would still be valuable in that they would refine all the materials that had previously been gone over rather hastily.

Q: You didn't have time to even think when you were in Pearl.

Captain Rochefort: No, the time in Pearl, say in '42, we

did not have time to think about, for example, the exact meaning or the exact pronunciation of some characters. We don't care about this. We just called these things what we had to, alpha, beta, delta, and gamma, and just let it go at that. We are not interested in the meaning. Later on, it might be of value--it would certainly be of interest--to have gotten the exact correct meaning of this as used by the Japanese.

Q: But nothing was revealed to you that was a blinding flash of light that you hadn't known about in general terms before you went into this group.

Captain Rochefort: Oh no, no. It would be, also, a lot of side effects of this thing, or as they say now in '69, there would be a lot of spin-offs, such as, whatever happened to one of our ships which we lost track of and which we called missing in action. This would be made available as part of this spin-off or this extra benefit. Basically the unit was organized again to perform strategic duties as opposed to tactical duties.

Q: And it was done before the end of the war when people didn't know how much they were going to need it in order for future operations.

Captain Rochefort: This would be a very handy thing to have had as a part of any overall intelligence organization, and a lot of information was made available. We, for example, lost some ships, and we didn't have any accurate information as to the cause of it. This would probably give us these. We could also use it by comparing reports emanating from the Japanese as the result of some battle or some engagement and compare those with the reports made by our own people. This would be very interesting, and which we found most interesting. Our people would, for example--their reports and this was doubtless a very conscientious report--their report of some action would vary considerably from the Japanese report. This would be rather interesting, too. This was the PSIS, and it should have been actually thought of some years ago and should have some years prior to when it was, and it should have been placed into effect. But, in any event, I think that was an indication of applied intelligence, and I think it served a useful purpose and I think it generated some information and possibly some thoughts. Strangely enough, I recall making one report which would be prior to the end of the war. This would be sometime in '45. I made a report dealing with Japanese submarine activities at the beginning of 1941 and extending on up to 1944, and I wished to send a copy of this to CinCPOA's Headquarters to the fleet intelligence officer and was directed by CominCh's representatives not to send such a report to CinCPOA.

Q: Why?

Captain Rochefort: No reason was given.

Q: Frustrating?

Captain Rochefort: No. I sent the report to CinCPOA.

Q: Oh, good for you.

Captain Rochefort: I don't know what the reason for that was, and I was not particularly interested, as a matter of fact, in the reason.

Q: But you thought that they ought to have it, so you saw that they got it.

Captain Rochefort: I saw that they had a copy of it, yes.

Q: Good. I'm pleased with you.

Captain Rochefort: Possibly misdirection of mail or something like this, but in any event they did get it so that's all of interest. Now that about completes this thing I would presume. Do you have any particular questions?

Q: I was going to make the comment that I know at one time

there was a recommendation for a commendation which you indicated Admiral King turned down, and yet I do note that you were awarded the Legion of Merit.

Captain Rochefort: Along with Joe Louis.[*] He received also a Legion of Merit.

Q: So you don't consider it a highly tangible...

Captain Rochefort: No, actually I don't hold with these things at all. I do not hold. As long as a person does what he considers to be an adequate job, or as long as he performs his duties to the best of his abilities, this is all the reward he needs.

Q: Oh, only partially.

Captain Rochefort: I do not particularly--and this certainly isn't sour grapes--I do not particularly subscribe to the theory of awarding a person a decoration merely because he had done an adequate job.

Q: Well, I think you did rather an adequate job, but my question was when Admiral King turned it down once, how come you did in fact receive it?

---

[*] The heavyweight boxing champion, who served in the Army during World War II.

Rochefort - 281

Captain Rochefort: No, I was recommended for the Distinguished Service Medal.

Q: Oh, and this is Legion of Merit. I see.

Captain Rochefort: Admiral Nimitz's idea and Admiral Bagley, who was in Com 14, on paper anyway was my immediate superior-- they both considered that a Legion of Merit would be awarded to some juniors, but as officer in charge I should be given a Distinguished Service Medal. This was overruled in CominCh's headquarters.

Q: You did go into that at some length in the other tape.

Captain Rochefort: The merits or demerits of this are not particularly important. It was rather interesting.

Q: Now when you were on general court-martial board, was that awaiting retirement?

Captain Rochefort: That was just awaiting retirement. That was the place where you'd ship these people to, just to get rid of them for temporary duty.

Q: But then you went back to active duty after three years, four years, as a member of the evaluation group on the staff commander in chief...

Captain Rochefort: Well, the problem there was--to be using just everyday language--the problem there was that after this attack from the North Koreans, it appeared quite probable there were going to be some serious repercussions from Congress as to the unpreparedness of the military, and it was considered on the Navy's part, as I understood this, that it would not be a bad idea to get the Navy's house in order and basically, as I understood it, the idea of the Fleet Evaluation Group, Pacific, which we used to call ValPac, was to determine how could we be so surprised, as we apparently were, by the attack of June 1950.

Q: That was going to be my question to you as to the level of intelligence in the fleet at that date.

Captain Rochefort: Well, that's it, and how can we avoid such a thing in the future?

Q: And that's what the purpose of this group was.

Captain Rochefort: That was the purpose of the group and accordingly, they organized a small group of people, some of whom were quite competent or quite experienced in, say, gunnery or supply or in operations or in planning and certainly in intelligence. Now, insofar as intelligence is concerned, obviously the people then on duty in responsible positions, including naval intelligence, including the fleet intelligence officer, Pacific, including the intelligence officer, ComNavFe.[*] These people would be automatically at least interested parties if not defenders in case some court-martial was going to result. Therefore, everybody had a sort of a vested interest in this thing and so could not be used. However, there's this fellow Rochefort still kicking around, and he still has some knowledge of fleet activities despite four years had gone by and he is still familiar with the general layout and the general personalities involved, and he has no axe to grind. He's not involved in it, because he's been on the retired list, so he's not involved in this thing directly. So maybe he should perform this duty insofar as intelligence is concerned. And, accordingly, I was asked if I would perform this service, which I was delighted to do. However we did--I did decide in the very beginning to leave out or not to discuss any facet relating to my previous duties such as radio intelligence or combat intelligence, whatever you wanted to call it--communication intelligence. We did not discuss this at all. But in the other duties, I was quite discouraged to find that although five years had passed since the end of World War II, that the level of intelligence--at least as it was practiced in the Pacific--was even more unacceptable than it would have been in 1941. In other words, nothing had been

---

[*]ComNavFe--Commander U.S. Naval Forces Far East.

accomplished. The three services were using different grid systems for reporting. It was a very unfortunate system of command relationships which probably could not have been greatly improved upon due to the presence of General MacArthur, but it was still more or less unacceptable.

Q: No improvements in equipment or...?

Captain Rochefort: Well, of course, I wasn't qualified to discuss anything like equipment or ships or personnel.

Q: I meant intelligence equipment.

Captain Rochefort: In intelligence, as far as I was concerned, it was not as desirable and not as efficient as it was in 1941. There were some notable exceptions to this. I recall the intelligence officer of the amphibious group was, in my opinion, quite qualified and extremely competent. Short of this, I very frankly was not impressed with the intelligence levels.

Q: Were there any recommendations you made which you think would be of value?

Captain Rochefort: Yes, I made several recommendations. On the first report that I prepared, I discussed the thing with the officer in charge of our group who was Admiral Moebus.* He directed me to discuss the matter with Admiral Radford, who was then CinCPac, as I recall.** I discussed it with him, and he ordered me to proceed independently of the other group and make my report directly to the Chief of Naval Operations, which I did through the Director of Naval Intelligence. I reported then directly to Director of Naval Intelligence. I was then ordered to return to Japan again as a member of the Fleet Evaluation Group for the purpose of seeing whether any of these recommendations or observations were actually being implemented.

Q: How long afterwards was that?

Captain Rochefort: This was immediately. I again proceeded to the Far East and spent an additional three or four months just repacing the ground. Some of these observations or suggestions, if you will, had been acted upon, but I could see no real improvement in the overall situation. And at this time, when I returned to Washington the second time, I suggested that I be placed on the retired list again, but I was told that they would prefer if I were still available, they would prefer it if I would remain in the vicinity of Washington in case my services were needed. The president of the Naval War College asked for my services as a translator or as an analyst of some description in preparation of studies

---

*Rear Admiral Lucian A. Moebus, USN.
**Admiral Arthur W. Radford, USN.

involving the World War II battles. I was engaged in this duty for several years, if I remember correctly. I asked for and was placed again on the inactive list in the spring of '53.

Q: March 1953.

Captain Rochefort: Yes, the spring of 1953. Subsequently, I remained on the inactive list.

Q: Did you feel you accomplished anything at the War College?

Captain Rochefort: Yes, it was most enjoyable duty, most enjoyable. It involved primarily translation of Japanese documents which the officer in charge of the project, who was Commodore Bates--as a result of his energy, he had a very adequate supply of captured Japanese documents that had been obtained both during the war and after the war.*
And I thoroughly enjoyed that duty and it was, I felt, quite worthwhile in attempting to prepare for the primary use of the War College as I understood it, a worthwhile study of individual battles and engagements--naval engagements--during World War II from the Japanese viewpoint as distinguished from books that were then being written and subsequently written which were--the kindest thing you can say about

---

*Following his retirement, Commodore Richard W. Bates was continued on active duty to make analyses of World War II battles for the Naval War College.

them was that they were just full of inaccuracies. This was the purpose of these studies, and we were engaged during that period of time I was there in an analysis of the Leyte operation. This is all we were engaged in--was the Leyte operation.

Q: Oh my, that was interesting though.

Captain Rochefort: Yes, it was very interesting and we devoted aproximately two years on that thing to the study of the Leyte operation.

Q: How did you come out with regard to Admiral Halsey?

Captain Rochefort: The concept of this study as developed by Commodore Bates was that one officer would be responsible for the Japanese side and another officer would be responsible for the analysis of the American side based on the information then available to the various commanders. And Commodore Bates would analyze both of these, and he was responsible for the preparation or recommendations, or suggestions regarding failures or non-failures on the part of both men so that I'm really not familiar with what final conclusions Commodore Bates came up with. I was only interested in the Japanese side which might be called a critique of Admiral Kurita's and other Japanese admirals' decisions were, based on what information they had when they made their decisions.

Q: How did you figure out that Kurita decided to advance backwards?

Captain Rochefort: This was very interesting. Actually, previous translations had--in my opinion, they were incorrect regarding why he turned back. I felt that considered at that time after some study of this that his reasons for turning back were not those which had generally been ascribed to him. His reasons were primarily to regroup his forces, to obtain additional information and determine what his future activities and actions should have been, and these then apparently convinced him that he--as long as he remained in the Pacific, eventually he would be run down and destroyed, and that must have been why he returned to San Bernardino Strait.

Q: It's a good thing that people make mistakes on both sides, isn't it?

Captain Rochefort: Yes, he arrived at this decision which was probably very sound, because at this time he then had been informed of what had happened to Admiral Shima[*] and the force coming through the Surigao Strait and what had happened to the other forces and what the situation was regarding land-based Japanese aircraft as well as what other forces would be available to him. As a result of this,

---

[*]Vice Admiral Kiyohide Shima, IJN.

then he returned north and retreated to San Bernardino Strait and he was narrowly missed by Halsey coming back from the north.

Q: I want to know what you are doing now, Captain, to bring us up to date.

Captain Rochefort: When I retired in '53, or re-retired in '53, like quite a few naval officers I was extremely critical of the way the government was being run and the way the money was being spent, particularly at the local level, and up to that point, of course, I had never even voted. So I began to take an interest in government as such with the result that I went down to city hall and volunteered for any kind of duty in my home town of Manhattan Beach [California] and volunteered for any kind of duty in which they wished to use me. They asked me to prepare some disaster plans for them to be used in event of natural disaster, war-caused disasters, major fires, and so on. I worked at that for a couple of years, and then additional cities asked me to perform the same duty. Eventually, this developed in 1957 and '58 with the organization of a group of 13 cities coordinating their disaster activities like pooling their forces and so on and so forth to obtain not only economy in form of money but also more efficiency. I believe that this has been extremely efficient. I believe that it has paid its way. As a result of combined budgets now, about one-third of what they were when I took over the job in 1957, and I'm still engaged in this duty. You might call it a consultant for disaster activities on the part of combined cities.

Q: But it's also a real contribution as a civic idea.

Captain Rochefort: I feel it is. Financially it has paid its way. Our budget today, for example, is a little less than it was ten years ago and I keep myself occupied to a degree involving activities in the event of both natural and war-caused disasters in developing what we call joint coordination on the part of these 13 cities involving maybe 700,000 people. I find it extremely interesting and well worthwhile. I'm still engaged in that and attempting to find a successor so that I can divest myself of all working activities, so far unsuccessfully.

Q: I hope it continues unsuccessfully because you shouldn't divest yourself of activity.

Captain Rochefort: I really enjoy this.

Q: Aren't you doing other things as a consultant where there are matters relating to intelligence?

Rochefort - 291

Captain Rochefort: Yes, but not officially and this would have to be on sort of an informal basis, particularly if it involved any governmental activities.

Q: What about the movie that you mentioned to me?

Captain Rochefort: That was merely a--what do you call these people? Adviser as to atmosphere or air or surroundings or something like this. That was merely the little minor activity. In this particular case, it dealt with discussions and use of classified material.

Q: Did you have to clear it with the Navy?

Captain Rochefort: No, actually some naval person came around in the midst of this and reminded me of the various security classifications. But in view of the fact that I considered myself very well aware of the need for security, having originated it actually some 30 or 40 years ago in the Navy Department, I told him that as far as I was concerned I was quite capable of guarding any government secrets.

Q: I'm sure you were.

Captain Rochefort: And possibly more so than he and his entire organization, and I was prepared to defend this as necessary, and I would be the sole judge of what required security measures and what did not require security measures. I have not heard from him since.

Q: I understand also that Kahn has written a book.*

Captain Rochefort: Kahn. I know who you mean. The <u>Code Breakers</u>.

Q: The <u>Code Breakers</u>. That you were told to have nothing to do with him.

Captain Rochefort: I had received, as I recall, several letters from Mr. Kahn, and he assured me that he had cleared this matter in the Navy Department. I also received about the same time a note, as I recall, from the Director of Naval Intelligence reminding me of security measures and suggesting the desirability of not being the subject of an interview with Mr. Kahn. I immediately replied, of course, and told the director that naturally I would comply with any request that he would have and I was notifying Mr. Kahn to that effect. I also told the Director of Naval Intelligence of any correspondence that I had had prior to that time and furnished him copies of it. Therefore, I had no further discussion with Mr. Kahn either then or later. My only connection with Mr. Kahn actually has been that he furnished

---

*David Kahn

me some extracts of his book and that was all.

Q: His book is out and very expensive.

Captain Rochefort: His book is out and is rather expensive. Insofar as my small contribution was concerned, I do not consider the book is particularly accurate, but I think he did a very good job. I do not know who he discussed this matter with or who he interviewed. I have no way of knowing that. But I would say that insofar as my small part in this whole thing is concerned that his remarks were not particularly accurate. It is still reasonable and would probably satisfy most of the readers.

Q: This brings up a question which I have been extremely interested in concerning as to why you do not write a book concerning your experiences.

Captain Rochefort: In the first place, I cannot write. Secondly, it would involve probably endless wrangles and hassles with the so-called security people at various levels who may be interested in security but probably more interested in protecting their own personal endeavors in this area, and it's just not worthwhile.

Q: You made the statement once before we started that writing it would cause trouble.

Captain Rochefort: It probably would cause trouble. It would probably irritate a lot of people. I think it would frighten some people who heretofore have enjoyed some type of reputation which is certainly not warranted, and I would believe it would not serve any useful purpose.

Q: Could you give me a for instance of what you were thinking about?

Captain Rochefort: Yes, if I were to be frank, for example, and write something in connection with this type of profession, if you will, or sub-profession, then I would have to be extremely critical of some people by name.

Q: Such as?

Captain Rochefort: Such as Masons, such as Redmans, such as Wengers, and other individuals. And I would not see that this would be to the advantage of the Navy. If I thought it were to the advantage of the Navy to prepare some sort of a factual account, then I would be the first one to do it.

Q: Don't you think it would be?

Captain Rochefort: No, I don't. I understand that the situation today is not particularly different than it was almost 30 years ago.

Q: Which would seem to me that the book then more needs writing.

Captain Rochefort: No, if I were asked by somebody in the Navy who is really interested in this sub-profession or who considered that it was to the interest of the Navy to write this sort of thing or to be a subject of an interview on the matter, I would be delighted to do it. But you'd have to convince me that this was in the best interest of the Navy.

Q: It would have to be a person, say, on active duty who is trying sincerely to get information from you to improve the situation not as a matter of gossip or chit-chat.

Captain Rochefort: Yes, I would not be interested in any gossip or anything of this nature. I would be interested in possibly suggesting or making some observations about the functions of various intelligence groups. How possibly they could be utilized to the best advantages. I have been informed, as I said previously, I understand and I think reliably informed that conditions today in certain aspects are not necessarily any better than they were 30 years ago. And 30 years ago they were not good. But with the war coming on, you don't have any time to change, but they could be changed now. I think the major difficulty is in appreciation of what intelligence is. I do not think that a majority of those in authority understand the functions of intelligence.

Q: Could you elaborate that?

Captain Rochefort: Yes. In intelligence it depends on what you're trying to do. Now as I've said repeatedly before, it has always been my opinion that intelligence as such is the providing of information to a military commander which is going to be of the nature telling him today what the probable enemy will do tomorrow. This is intelligence at its best. Now to do this, of course, you have to have a lot of material. You have to have a fairly good organization-- not a large organization but a good organization including good reference materials. For example, we used to have within the Navy, and the Army had the same thing--a set of books called monographs. Now these were a collection of information--topographical, personalities, restrain areas, all sorts of things, fiscal, financial, agricultural. This is supposed to give you background of what this nation requires or needs or has. This thing became a joke actually. These monograph things became a joke. I had, and still have as a matter of fact, a set of British counterparts which were prepared during the interval between World War I and World War II. These are infinitely superior to that we had--infinitely superior.

Q: Were they prepared by intelligence people?

Captain Rochefort: They were prepared mostly by scholars in England. As a matter of fact, I've used those since the war. A set of those was made available to me by the British during World War II, and I found them very useful. This is just one phase. Now in order to perform the intelligence functions properly, you have to become involved in all sorts of background material such as, good soundings in all ports, currents, tides, any navigational things. You have to be informed of personalities involved such as, what sort of a type person was this Admiral Yamamoto and that sort of thing. You have to have this. You have to, or should have, a very highly developed radio intelligence or combat--whatever you prefer to call this--communication intelligence organization and, most important of all would be the chain of command. Intelligence is not particularly liked by the average American person. It is not particularly liked by, for example, senior naval officers or certainly senior Army officers. Well, the reason for this is that we abhor anything regarding snooping or spying. Wasn't it a Secretary of State that said when they closed up the Black Chamber in say 1928 or '29--wasn't it Secretary of State that said that gentlemen do not read other people's mail?*

Q: Yes, it was.

Captain Rochefort: Well, he doesn't know very much about intelligence.

Q: I would think also you would have to understand operations, fleet operations.

Captain Rochefort: An intelligence officer should in the case of the Navy alone, just referring merely to the Navy. This fellow should be a naval officer first and an intelligence officer second.

Q: I think you made that point so well, and it's worth repeating because Friedman, whose name came up because of his recent death, and Safford--you spoke of both of them as being extremely fine technicians but without the background of operations which would make them unable to operate as an intelligence officer as expressed by your philosophy. Am I correct?

---

*This remark is widely attributed to Henry L. Stimson when he became Secretary of State in 1929.

Captain Rochefort: I think that's phrasing it very well. It depends of course on how you look at this intelligence problem. Intelligence has always been a sort of a laughable thing, at least within the Navy. It was a place where if people wanted to go to duty in Washington and they had money, then they would wind up in intelligence because you don't do any work in intelligence. It just was a nice social job. You get to see various embassies. You're invited to various parties at various embassies or legations or one thing and another, and you mix with nice people, but you don't do anything. This is intelligence.

Q: You mean this is a concept that uninformed people have.

Captain Rochefort: Well, these are probably a majority of people we've had serving in intelligence.

Q: Oh so?

Captain Rochefort: Yes. The only exception to this I think would probably be those people involved in oriental areas such as China and Japan, particularly Japan. These people really have had a concept of what is intelligence. It depends actually on what you're talking about. If you're talking about being able to balance a tea cup nicely or play the guitar or know the right people or to be able to talk

intelligently to other nations, this is one thing. If your
concept involves a presenting to your commanding officer
information that he can use with a degree of acceptability
and dealing with future operations based on knowledge not
based on what the newspapers said or will say, this is something
else again. And I've always felt that this is the great
weakness in our concept. I understand it still is. For
example, I think I mentioned one time the CIA--I was told
by a CIA person in 1950 in Korea that the CIA had predicted
this attack in June of 1950 and had prepared actually an
estimate of what would probably happen. Unfortunately,
they did not pass this estimate on, and they did not distribute
it, and therefore the whole effort was completely fruitless.
And I would not even dignify this by calling it intelligence,
because intelligence to be of value to your commander must
be placed in his hands in sufficient time for him to act on it
and I think I also mentioned that during the initial Guadalcanal
operation I conceived that in connection say, with the Tokyo
Express and another operation similar to that, that we had
to place in the hands of Admiral Halsey in sufficient time
for him to act on it information regarding the operations
of the Tokyo Express. And if we were unable to give him
information in time for him to act on it, I refused to let
that leave our office because he will know about this afterwards.
Afterwards he knows all about it, so there isn't any point
in telling him this.

Q: If you wrote your book, would you find yourself being critical of Admiral Nimitz?

Captain Rochefort: No. No, because I feel that this is not to place myself naturally on the level with Admiral Nimitz, but the best thing--possibly the best thing that ever happened to the Navy during the war was Nimitz's acceptance of Station Hypo's estimates of what the Japanese were going to do, not only at Coral Sea but at Midway and subsequent. He acted on this, for which I am forever grateful, somewhat respectfully grateful, to Admiral Nimitz.

Q: Did you feel any bitterness toward him when he did not back you up at your experience in Washington though?

Captain Rochefort: Oh no, no. Not in the slightest, because he made his decision. He apparently was willing to back Station Hypo up to a point.

Q: But I mean when you had your personal difficulties in Washington and he was made aware of them, do you have any criticism that he didn't support you?

Captain Rochefort: Oh no, no. Because this is a decision that he had to make.

Q: Based on factors that you may not be aware of.

Captain Rochefort: Based on factors that I might not be aware of and based on some possibly overriding factors. This thing pertaining to me or pertaining to the Station Hypo was a relatively minor matter. Now it might personally affect me, possibly disadvantageously, but this had nothing whatever to do with the larger picture. So whatever happens to me and whatever happens at the station, whatever happens to any of the other people, this could very well be secondary to his major problems. Oh, no, no, I would never consider anything like this. And of course, I contributed to some of these things too myself on my own motion.

Q: You have taken full responsibility, I think.

Captain Rochefort: Yes, I take full responsibility for what happened and my only regret was, and still is, as a matter of fact, that I had been able to, say, swallow my pride, I could possibly have been of further help to the Navy. Possibly. And I could have possibly been more loyal to my subordinates by not deserting them in the middle of everything.

Q: At Station Hypo...

Captain Rochefort: Yes, when I was running Station Hypo. I might possibly have been able to contribute a little bit more or perhaps I would have been more effective rather than running around organizing some intelligence center in San Francisco or in command of some floating drydock.

Q: It seems such an almost--well, I would like to think of a nice word--at least contradictory assignment from one which was so extremely important.

Captain Rochefort: Yes, that's my only regret. I should have accepted the situation and subordinated my own wishes. I've always regretted subsequently that I didn't do so.

Q: Speaking of, which we are, of publications, do you consider Walter Lord's book, The Incredible Victory, as being authentic? I'm speaking now of how he described Station Hypo.

Captain Rochefort: Insofar as my activities are concerned, I think he did an excellent job. I think it is very factual. I could of course resent such things as the smoking jacket and things like this, but I think he put this in there for atmosphere or color and I don't object to this actually at all. The real reason, as I've said before, was mainly because I was cold.

Q: The thing that was really important though that you told me and put on the tape, he didn't tell the fact of your use of the IBM cards in the millions and...

Captain Rochefort: Well, I considered this was sort of a technical matter and it didn't add anything to Mr. Lord's book.

Q: You thought he was too soft on Theobald, you said.*

Captain Rochefort: I thought he was too soft on several senior officers, and I still think so, but you must remember here again that Mr. Lord is not writing the book to antagonize people. He's writing the book for posterity which is accurate insofar as the facts are concerned, but he is still not interested in destroying someone's reputation.

Q: You said that your feeling was that Theobald was afraid of the Japs.

Captain Rochefort: Theobald. "Fuzzy" Theobald.

Q: Yes.

Captain Rochefort: Well, I did not know Admiral Theobald

---

*Rear Admiral Robert A. Theobald, USN.

particularly well. I'd been in contact with him and observed him. He would not be my idea of a task force commander.

Q: Hadn't you given him information of the Japs' capabilities and intentions which he ignored?

Captain Rochefort: No, more than that. We had furnished this information to Admiral Nimitz who in turn had furnished it to his commanders so that you might more properly say that Admiral Theobald had been informed and instructed by Admiral Nimitz, not by me. He doesn't have to pay any attention to me. But he should have paid attention to Admiral Nimitz. But it would be something like I recall when Admiral Ghormley came through Pearl to take command of this force which was later to be known as the Guadalcanal operation--when he came through Pearl, his communication officer--I've forgotten his name now--came to me and asked me, said that he had heard by the grapevine that we had a little organization out there and therefore as the communications officer for Admiral Ghormley, he would be very much interested in possibly receiving some information from us or possibly some personnel that he could use advantageously. He discussed the matter with Admiral Turner, who was going to be one of the task force commanders for Admiral Ghormley.

Q: Turner?

Captain Rochefort: Richmond Kelly Turner.

Q: Oh yes.

Captain Rochefort: R.K. Turner, and he was informed very bluntly by Admiral Turner that he didn't need any of this so-called goddamn foolishness by these people. He was perfectly prepared to handle his own problems. Admiral Turner was. Well, this is somewhat debatable but anyway. I think here this would illustrate the feeling of a lot of people, including people like Admiral Ghormley or Admiral Turner, that they are not particularly interested in this thing called intelligence.

Q: And yet it was one of the--I think of all of the conversations of people who had described Nimitz, Admiral Nimitz, was his ability to take every possible factor that could be to his advantage and use it, and intelligence was one of those things.

Captain Rochefort: Yes. Regardless of the reasons, whether it was as a result of the urgings by Admiral Nimitz's staff or members of his staff, whether it is due to Admiral Nimitz's brilliance or whatever the reason was, Admiral Nimitz chose to accept our estimate of what was going to happen rather than the estimate of CominCh, Admiral King, or certainly of the Army. Whatever the reason was, you can ascribe--I didn't know actually Admiral Nimitz particularly well, I was never privileged to discuss things with him. He chose to work through his own staff which, of course, is proper. And therefore he would get his intelligence information from his fleet intelligence officer rather than from me, which would be quite proper. It was up to me to keep the fleet intelligence officer informed as to what I thought.

Q: You also spoke of Morison's series of books as being whitewash.*

Captain Rochefort: Well, here again is just a personal view. Admiral Morison--I recall, I think, meeting him just once while I was still out in Pearl and also I was advised by CinCPac staff that I was to have no dealings with Admiral Morison. He was not to be allowed in my place.

Q: This was out in Pearl?

Captain Rochefort: Yes. I would conceive--and again this is a personal estimate and probably biased--that Admiral Morison's main function in writing these books was to defend the administration.

Q: Roosevelt had chosen him to be the historian?

---

*Rear Admiral Samuel Eliot Morison's 15-volume History of United States Naval Operations in World War II.

Rochefort - 308

Captain Rochefort: He was the court historian, if you will, or something like this. I do not think just cursory reading of several of his books--I do not think these things were particularly accurate and they obviously should have been written by somebody who had quite a knowledge of not only writing ability, but they should have had some naval experience or some experience of Navy things.

Q: They are always referred to as source material.

Captain Rochefort: Sure they are and Sam is--well, as I told somebody in Newport that asked me to just glance over one of the drafts of one of the manuscripts for, I think, Leyte which I was in working, and I made the remark after reading this draft over that I could produce at least one error in fact on every page of the book.

Q: Error of fact?

Captain Rochefort: Error in fact, yes. I could produce one error in fact on every page--at least one. No, I think if there is such a thing as history, then I think these things go down in history as something less than the final authority on any particular matter that is involved in writing. No, I mean this is not any criticism of one person. You write a book for some reason. Now, there has been a rash of books come out, of course, about the making of a president and the unmaking of the president. Well, these are written for various purposes and not all of them are written for strictly academic reasons. They're just written for some other purpose which you've just got to accept.

Q: You spoke of Admiral Zacharias, also, and his work on psychological warfare in the Pacific.* We are having a session on book reviews, I guess.

Captain Rochefort: Yes. As Zacharias explained it to me in Washington, he believed that if he could develop a psychological warfare capability within the United States with particular reference to the Japanese, this would serve a very useful purpose in possibly shortening the war and certainly saving lives, etc. and etc. But I think that Admiral Zacharias, as I told him at the time, was operating under a misconception. In the first place, the Japanese individuals did not have access to a radio and this psychological warfare effort would be devoted primarily through the radio and appealing to the individuals or the individual naval officers or the individual naval people. But the fallacy here is that all during the Thirties--the Twenties and the Thirties and certainly prior to the war and during the war-- the Japanese individuals were only permitted to have radios

---

*Rear Admiral Ellis M. Zacharias, USN.

if they had a license from the police and not too many Japanese had radios and that certainly they would not be permitted to have radios if in the judgment of the government, the military personnel of the government, if these radios could be used for reading broadcasts or listening to broadcasts emanating from non-Japanese sources. The Japanese are not going to miss this opportunity. And that even if you did know and knew intimately some Japanese officer that he had met socially before either in Washington or in Tokyo, even if he did know these people, they are not going to abide by his desires if, particularly, they conflicted with the Japanese Government policy. Merely because you met somebody and this fellow is an acquaintance and you tell him, say in 1944, "Look, Bud, you can't win. Why don't you quit because I, Zacharias, advise you to do so." This I doubt would have very little influence on that person's decisions.

Q: Weren't you told at one time, also, that in taking a job he shouldn't be permitted on the premises, so to speak?

Captain Rochefort: Yes, I had been directed by at least two commanders that Zacharias was a persona non grata.

Q: Yet he was so well-known. The name is practically known by any person who would think of naval intelligence.

Captain Rochefort: This is correct but this really has

nothing whatever to do with the fact of it. He was well-known, but a lot of people have been well-known. I recall some person had a big reputation involving air-borne troops in World War II in Europe who was supposed to have invented a couple of expressions such as "Oh nuts" or something like that. As it later developed during the tenure of Eisenhower, it develops that this fellow's views are not necessarily good. You can build your own reputation if you want. There's no problem here. So that I have an unfortunate habit of judging people by their last record or achievement. For example, you show me a person who has made many predictions in the past or performed any duties in the past or has made many recommendations in the past, and he has uniformly turned out to be poor. I do not place much reliance on that fellow's recommendations today.

Q: I concur most heartily. He's not going to all of a sudden start making brilliant recommendations if his pattern in the past has been poor.

Captain Rochefort: For example, we have a fellow--I'll just pick a name out of the hat--we'll call him Arthur B. Schlesinger, Jr. And his main claim to fame seems to be that he was a Pulitzer Prize winner. Well, I don't think this is any particular reason for somebody standing up in front of the world and claiming to be a great, big expert.

Because I remember a fellow who got the Nobel Prize one year by the name of Martin Luther King, and I would think that he was the last person who would get a peace prize by reason of the fact that he stirred up all this trouble in the United States. I'm not questioning his motives or whether it was a valid thing or not. But merely because you might give him a war prize but never a peace prize. That's beside the point.

Q: That's a matter of opinion, too.

Captain Rochefort: However, you take a fellow named Schlesinger and I just picked this name out of the hat. It could be anybody else who has some sort of a reputation among certain groups of people as being somewhat literate and somewhat scholarly and yet I would remind you that this fellow was involved in the Bay of Pigs. Well, if he starts recommending some military action, I would think to myself, "Now, wait a minute. What's the track record on this fellow?" It's just unfortunate this way.

Q: I would think that this is always true, and I always talk to young people that way when they are talking about being guided by someone, to say, "What's their experience? What's their record? Have they been right most of the time or wrong?" Then decide should they be a good person to guide them.

Captain Rochefort: That's correct. We are sort of idol-worshippers around here, and these idols are sometimes built by one person's own estimate of himself. He just built himself up.

Q: Have we mentioned Yamamoto? I know that his plane was shot down and he was killed because of intelligence indicating that his arrival at a certain place and he came. Was Hypo involved in that?

Captain Rochefort: That I do not know. That was after I had left. It could have been an operation by people down in Australia which we called Bellconner. It could have been their work alone. It could have been Hypo's work alone. It could actually have been Negat which was the Washington place. I would be inclined to say that Negat had nothing to do with it, merely because they were not at the tactical level. They were not working in terms of minutes. They were working in terms of days or weeks or months. I would say that my best guess would be it would be either Hypo or a combination of Hypo and Bell that produced the information. I was told that there was some discussion of this matter and it was actually a difference of opinion. Some people in Pearl considered that no action was indicated, don't shoot this fellow down because of the danger of the source of the information being made public. This would have a big bearing on the subject. And secondly, that we know, probably we have a pretty fair idea--we probably know what Admiral Yamamoto would do in a given situation. We know this by now. Now, if you kill this guy off, you are going to have another commander in chief. We don't know much about this guy and this would be balanced against the value of shooting down the commander in chief, just killing the commander in chief. You have to balance these two things together. I've been told by people that were present and involved in this thing that there was a difference of opinion on the action that was taken and it was finally resolved at Washington either by CominCh or by the President or by someone else directing that efforts be made to shoot this fellow down.

Q: We had two other items--I don't want to keep you too long.

Captain Rochefort: We're on the second half now.

Q: Shall we stop?

Captain Rochefort: No, just wind the whole thing up.

Q: I just wanted to ask you about your two comments that we had mentioned when the tape was not running of information intelligence, one about Wake Island and one about Rabaul, in which you had furnished intelligence.

Captain Rochefort: Well, Rabaul--this was, of course, before we got what I refer to as the first team in action. This is when we are still dealing with the--for want of a better name--peacetime admirals. We are dealing with these people and they have still not developed the winning combination.

Q: It's after Pearl but before Nimitz?

Captain Rochefort: Yes. Well, Nimitz is actually the commander in chief at this time. He was CinCPac at this time. You see, he took over at about the time of the Roberts Commission.

Q: Christmas Day, I think it was.

Captain Rochefort: Christmas Eve or Christmas or something.

Q: Or New Year's Eve or some such day as that.

Captain Rochefort: And in the interim, of course, you had the remnants of Admiral Kimmel's staff and of Admiral Pye.[*] For good and sound reason, you've got to relieve Kimmel on the spot--for good and sound reasons. We still haven't

---

[*] Admiral William S. Pye, USN, was acting Commander in Chief Pacific Fleet during the latter part of December 1941.

got time to get somebody out from Washington, so this naturally is going to take a little time, measured in days maybe. So in the interim, Admiral Pye is the next senior in the fleet. I think Admiral Pye was Commander Battle Force. He then was made this acting thing so that he was actually in command during the interim between Kimmel and the arrival of Nimitz. So you naturally have some confusion, because you're going to have different staffs, and different parts of different staffs. Admiral Pye would of course want to bring his chief of staff, who as I recall was Captain Train.*
And when you've got people like Admiral Draemel, who I believe was in destroyers, and you have Admiral Theobald who I think had Scouting Force Destroyers, and people like this. You still have these people and this, of course, makes for nothing but confusion which we had to suffer through for a while until the arrival at least of Admiral Nimitz. And it took Admiral Nimitz some appreciable time, of course, to select his own commanders. He couldn't do this just overnight. So we had during this interval what I would choose to call a second team and it took us some months to develop the first team. During this time is when we had some decisions made which are the least bit questionable. But which you would probably expect because you've got a general upheaval here.

Q: But you had furnished intelligence concerning both of these incidents?

---
*Captain Harold C. Train, USN, Battle Force chief of staff.

Captain Rochefort: We had furnished intelligence and as I recall, we furnished intelligence several days after Pearl to the effect that parts, some units of the Kido Butai, which had been the unit that attacked at Pearl--several units of this force were ordered to make an attack on Wake which had resisted several earlier attacks by Japanese forces in the Marshalls. We furnished this information to CinCPac and it was my understanding at the time, which was purely second-hand, because I did not know and I did not want to know and I didn't need to know what plans CinCPac was developing. I was interested, naturally, but it was no concern of mine, so I preferred not to know again on the theory that the fewer people that know about an operation the safer it's going to be. But I was under the impression that this matter was given serious consideration and in fact several carriers were ordered out there in the vicinity of Wake so that if an attack was made by a couple of Japanese carriers, then, and if an opportunity presented itself for our carriers to attack the Japanese carriers while their planes were at Wake that possibly we would have a great opportunity to destroy these carriers. This operation was called off, either by--it depends on who you're talking to--either by the people at Pearl or by orders from Washington, and did not want to risk losing any more vessels.

Q: That would have been Pye in Pearl or Short in Washington.

Captain Rochefort: No, either King--Admiral King or Admiral--Chief of Naval Operations, Stark.[*]

Q: I meant Stark or Pye.

Captain Rochefort: It depends on who you are talking to and I actually would not be prepared to--because all my information was obviously second-hand.

Q: But you had given intelligence so that they knew where these carriers were to be and what their operation was?

Captain Rochefort: We had furnished information which we thought was very good. Actually there was very little risk involved in this, because the Japanese at that time had no knowledge of the location of any of our carriers, and I'm reasonably sure that if they had just detached two carriers to attack Wake, to sort of subdue Wake, that any hostile action on our part by way of our two carriers would have been a tremendous surprise to them and probably would have been successful, probably it would have been. But in any event, this whole operation was called off.

Q: The books say that that was the cause of more depression in Pearl, at least almost as much as the bombing.

---

[*] Admiral Harold R. Stark, USN.

Rochefort - 319

Captain Rochefort: Yes, it seemed to be. Some people were a little bit discouraged at this, as they were kind of discouraged for succeeding weeks--weekends, I should say--when they would get a message from Washington reminding them that the Japanese were noted for being somewhat treacherous by attacking on Sunday.

Q: Not really.

Captain Rochefort: No, it's not true at all but this...

Q: Did they get continuing messages on the weekend?

Captain Rochefort: Yes, reminding us--on holidays and things like that. Well, this comes under the heading of covering your number. This is what it really does and it gets a little bit discouraging to have people, your own superiors sometimes, reminding you that this, that, and the other can happen. Sure it can happen. We all know this. But there isn't any point in reminding you other than in the event that something does happen and these other people--I told him so. This is kind of ridiculous actually.

Q: At that point, after the fact. One last question and then I'll let you go. You made the comment that Ingersoll should have had the job instead of Nimitz.*

Captain Rochefort: Did I ever say that?

Q: Yes.

Captain Rochefort: Well, I shouldn't have said that. No, because, of course, I'm obviously not qualified to say who should or who should not have been. This depends on a variety of factors. I had the privilege of serving under Admiral Ingersoll, Royal Ingersoll, as a cruiser commander, cruiser division commander, and I was personally quite impressed with Admiral Ingersoll, but he did have one failing which was told to me by several of his superiors at the time. That he was never one for tooting his own horn and therefore would probably never get a job.

Q: Is that so?

Captain Rochefort: Yes. I don't--there was never any question about his ability, but he did not go around telling everybody how good he was. He was very self-effacing, very quiet, he was very pleasant, he was never a bully as some people were and therefore would probably not go too far, just merely

---

*Rear Admiral Royal Ingersoll, USN, was Assistant Chief of Naval Operations at the time of the attack on Pearl Harbor. He soon relieved Admiral King as Commander in Chief Atlantic Fleet.

Rochefort - 321

because of that.

Q: I never read anything about the maneuverings that proceeded as a result of Admiral Nimitz being selected.

Captain Rochefort: Well, I was told by some people that at the time, that Admiral Nimitz was Chief of Bureau of Naval Personnel and of course the President was vitally concerned with naval personnel. It was one of his hobbies, you might say. And there was reason to assume that he and Admiral Nimitz, as Chief of Bureau of Naval Personnel, would probably have met more often in connection with naval personnel matters than he would have say with Bureau of Medicine and Surgery or Bureau of Construction and Repair and things like this. And the President was favorably impressed with Admiral Nimitz as a result of their various meetings prior to December 7th dealing with personnel. That's what I was told. He was favorably impressed with this particular Chief of the Bureau and this probably had a lot to do with his selection. It could not have been--I have no way of knowing.

Q: Well, your comments about yourself are certainly enlightening and several comments that you made about Admiral Nimitz, I think, are interesting, particularly the time when you told about the conference when they wanted to keep the planes there and they said, "Well, the Saratoga is coming in" and it wasn't until later that it was going to be there for 20 minutes.

Captain Rochefort: You'd never guess this by looking at him, but Admiral Nimitz obviously had a very deep sense of humor. You would think this was kind of strange in the midst of a war, a very important war. But Admiral Nimitz apparently had--some people used to refer to him as the dumb Dutchman and some people--and again this is secondhand--some people such as Secretary Forrestal did not like Admiral Nimitz as Commander in Chief Pacific.*

Q: Or Spruance, either one.

Captain Rochefort: No, they didn't like Spruance either, because he was a similar man, similar type. He said very little. He was actually colorless. He wasn't the flamboyant type, he didn't go around with pistols on his hip or anything like this. He just was given an assignment--I'm referring to Admiral Spruance now--he was given an assignment. He performed these duties adequately as a naval officer and he would probably have been the most surprised person in the world if you referred to this fellow as a genius or a hero or anything else. He was merely performing the duties that had been assigned to him by Admiral Nimitz. Admiral

----
*James V. Forrestal, after serving as Under Secretary, became Secretary of the Navy in 1944.

Nimitz similarly was performing his duties as commander in chief to the best of his ability and he turned out a very adequate job. Now you can wax heroic about this. You say this man should be compared with Lord Nelson and somebody else. You can do this if you want to. But I'm sure in Admiral Nimitz's view he was merely doing as I used to say he was merely doing what he was paid to do, which is to win the battle. And this is what he was hired to do and this is what he should have done.

Q: Well, we were lucky in the nation that he was there being hired to do it.

Captain Rochefort: Very fortunate. Very fortunate. Both he and Admiral Spruance and in another sense, of course, Admiral Halsey, and in another sense, the fellow piloting the airplane or commanding the submarine. These people all performed their duties and did a real good job so, as a result, we won the war.

Q: And the nation which backed it up and the people who came on as reservists and everybody else.

Captain Rochefort: They all did their job the best they could. I don't object at all to saying what I think about an individual. This is my personal view. Nor would I object to somebody making some critical observation about me and my rather lowly position. I'll accept this. I mean, I don't get mad about this. If you can't take this, as President Truman said, then you get out of the kitchen.

Q: If you can't stand the heat, get out of the kitchen.

Captain Rochefort: But rather than award somebody for doing a fair job or an average job or even an adequate job--instead of awarding people like this you should say, you did a pretty fair job, and just let it go at that. You don't want to give a Medal of Honor for this business. This is not called for. So the lad gets killed. Well, he's either a little bit slow thinking by jumping on this grenade, maybe saving six or seven other people, but chances are that his brain wasn't functioning, otherwise he'd have run in the other direction. So we give a Medal of Honor for this. Well, so the guy gets awarded for doing something that if he had a quicker mind he wouldn't have done. Just another way of looking at this thing. Well, like Sergeant York, if Sergeant York had any brains at all in World War I, you don't ever go charging up some goldarned hill to knock out a machine gun nest because you're going to get killed if you do this.[*] Why not wait for the airplane or somebody to come back and do the job for you.

Q: Well, it's been just real interesting and Mr. Mason

---

[*] Army Medal of Honor winner Alvin York.

said he hoped that when you got the manuscript that you wouldn't change it or delete anything.

Captain Rochefort: No, unless I've made some remark about some individual which is really uncalled for. That would be my only thing.

Q: But he said that he appreciated your expansiveness and that you were willing to talk about your days.

Captain Rochefort: Well, if it's going to do the service any good, this would be the whole criteria. If it's going to do the service any good, I would be very glad to say that. But if it's not going to be for the good of the service or if it's to vent my personal spleen, then I don't want to say anything. This is the way I feel about the thing.

Q: Well, thank you.

INDEX

CAPTAIN JOSEPH J. ROCHEFORT

Army Air Forces
  When presented with the information that a second Japanese attack on Pearl Harbor was imminent in early 1942, claimed that their planes would be of no use for defense, pp. 206, 208; Nimitz's solution to their reluctance to send their few remaining planes from Oahu to Midway in mid-1942, pp. 227-229; disparity in ship sinkings claimed and what could be verified in the early 1940s, pp. 244-246.

Bell
  see Station Bell(conner), Australia

Carpender, Lieutenant Commander Arthur S., USN (USNA, 1908)
  Rochefort's assessment of hard-driving perfectionist as commanding officer of the destroyer Macdonough (DD-331) in the mid-1920s, pp. 49-50.

Cast
  see Station Cast; Cavite, The Philippines

Coral Sea, Battle of (May, 1942)
  In reponse to request from Admiral King for estimation of future Japanese plans, Station Hypo gave first prediction of action at Coral Sea immediately after attack on Pearl Harbor, p. 174; information about Japanese movement towards Coral Sea circulated among U.S. ships in the spring of 1942 without their knowing the source, p. 181; deductions made by Station Hypo to provide intelligence about Japanese plans, pp. 189-90, 196-197; intelligence generated by Stations Cast, Bell, and Hypo before Coral Sea judged by Rochefort to be better than that offered before action at Midway in 1942, p. 237.

Cryptanalysis
  Rochefort's introduction to in the mid-1920s, pp. 5-8; different types of systems, p. 8; Army's involvement before Navy during World War I, pp. 8-9; development of Navy's organization under Safford in the early 1920s, pp. 10-11; Navy's Washington organization under Rochefort in the mid-1920s, pp. 14, 27-32, 38-39, 41-43; basics of solving codes, pp. 14-15, 17-18, 20-21, 140-141; Navy's organization under communications control but worked jointly with intelligence, pp. 18-19, 99; Rochefort's assessment of personality necessary for a cryptanalyst, pp. 12-14, 33-36, 46-47; Army-Navy cooperation in the 1920s, pp. 42-43, few advances in the field during the 1930s, pp. 79-80, 102; importance of careful translation to operation, pp. 105-110; system used at Station Hypo in the early 1940s, pp. 127-137; shift of importance from Washington office to Pearl Harbor after 7 December 1941, pp. 116-117, 119, 140-145; Rochefort's recommendations for training and organization of personnel, pp. 149, 212-213,

295-296; use of fake or deceptive signals by Japan, Germany, and the United States in World War II, pp. 166-167; Rochefort felt it important not to get too much information on what the U.S. was doing to keep it from coloring translations, p. 188; failure at Pearl Harbor, pp. 110-114, 116, 235-237, 239; failures in Guadalcanal Campaign in the fall of 1942, pp. 240-242, 265, 300, 305-306.

Downes, Lieutenant Commander Oliver L., USN (USNA, 1913)
   Commanding officer of the destroyer USS Macdonough (DD-331), considered by Rochefort to be a "Naval Academy type," p. 52.

Driscoll, Mrs. Agnes M.
   Very capable cryptanalyst in Navy's Washington office whom Rochefort considers largely responsible for first Japanese code broken, pp. 29-31.

Dyer, Lieutenant Commander Thomas H., USN (USNA, 1924)
   Assigned to Station Hypo in the early 1940s, pp. 13, 32, 103; kept no-doze pills on his desk during major operations to help sustain the staff during 20-hour days, pp. 124-125; installed first IBM system at Station Hypo, pp. 128, 157-158.

Fleet Evaluation Group, Pacific (ValPac)
   Study group tasked with determining why the United States was caught unprepared by North Korean attack in June of 1950, pp. 282-283; Rochefort makes recommendations through the Director of Naval Intelligence and is sent to Japan to check on their implementation in the early 1950s, pp. 284-285.

Friedman, William
   As reserve army officer, started in cryptanalysis during World War I and was in charge of the Army's organization in the mid-1920s; wrote the primary reference book on the subject for use by all units, pp. 8-9, 40-41, 43-44.

Frost, Commander Holloway H., USN (USNA, 1910)
   Very capable navigator of the battleship USS California (BB-44), a battle force flagship in the 1930s, who considered this position minor compared to his other simultaneous professional undertakings, pp. 49-52.

Guadalcanal, British Solomon Islands
   In August of 1942 a U.S. marine unburies a code book hidden by Japanese prior to their hasty retreat, with the negative effect of prompting a new code by the enemy, pp. 118-119.

Hart, Admiral Thomas C., USN (USNA, 1897)
   While in San Francisco in connection with a Pearl Harbor inquiry in the mid-1940s contacted Rochefort, and despite his protests triggered his return to duty in Washington, p. 268.

Holmes, Lieutenant Wilfred J., USN (USNA, 1922)
  During duty at Station Hypo in the early 1940s in charge
  of charts and maps, p. 127; provided daily Japanese ship
  plots to LCDR Layton, Fleet Intelligence Officer on Admiral
  Nimitz's staff in 1942, p. 180; Rochefort assesses as not
  familiar with Japanese language or mores, but experienced
  with ship plotting, p. 218.

Hypo
  see Station Hypo; Pearl Harbor, Hawaiian Islands

Indianapolis, USS (CA-35)
  Rochefort's opinion that the sinking of this heavy cruiser
  by the Japanese in July of 1945 was a failure of cryptologists,
  pp. 239-240.

Ingersoll, Rear Admiral Royal E., USN (USNA, 1905)
  Rochefort's assessment after serving under him in the late
  1930s is that he was an extremely capable leader but
  with a fatal flaw for a flag officer--modesty, pp. 319-320.

Intelligence
  Reaction of senior naval officers to information provided
  by cryptanalysis during World War II, pp. 22, 25-26,
  176, 179, 192, 219-220, 296, 304-307; difficulties in
  retaining secrecy about codebreaking ability during World
  War II, pp. 22-25, 37, 42-43, 101, 118-119; ability to
  verify or discard claims of ship losses, pp. 244-246;
  Joint Intelligence Center, Pacific Ocean Area, p. 246;
  information provided by Station Hypo foiled Japanese
  reconnaissance effort between attacks on Pearl Harbor
  and Midway, pp. 246-247; Rochefort's assessment of the
  function of intelligence, p. 296; upon Rochefort's return
  to active duty in 1950, his disappointment with the quality
  of intelligence which he feels is worse than in 1941,
  pp. 283-284.

Japan
  U.S. naval officers attached to the embassy in the 1920s
  and 1930s to learn Japanese language and mores, pp. 60-66,
  73-74; attitudes concerning war and honor prior to World
  War II, pp. 66-68, 75; US-Japan relations prior to World
  War II, pp. 68-71, 75-76; influence of the Japanese army
  and navy on the emperor in the 1930s, pp. 74-76; Rochefort's
  assessment of Japanese errors at Pearl Harbor, pp. 170-172;
  Kido Butai (Japanese striking force), pp. 173-174, 248-249,
  317; Rochefort's thoughts on why they did not attack
  U.S. mainland during World War II, pp. 192-193; Rengo
  Kantai (combined fleet), p. 248; at Battle of Midway
  in June of 1942, pp. 248-250.

discussion of "red", "purple" codes, p. 135; use of two or three letter codes to represent locations, example: AH meant Pearl Harbor, pp. 198-203, 211; operational order of 20 May 1942, translated by Station Hypo on 25 May, gave information on proposed Midway attack, pp. 215-217; code changed after 20 May transmission; new code broken by August, 1942, pp. 242-243.

Jersey, Lieutenant Commander Chester C., USN (USNA, 1910)
Met Rochefort while both were stationed aboard the USS Cuyama (AO-3) in the early 1920s, later brought Rochefort to duty in Washington and introduced him to cryptography, pp. 5, 7.

Joint Intelligence Center, Pacific Ocean Area (JICPOA)
Formerly Intelligence Center, Pacific Ocean Area (ICPOA), established in the mid-1940s to coordinate all phases of military intelligence; greatly eased problems caused by disparity of reported kills to actual sinkings, pp. 246, 256.

Kahn, David
While doing research for his book about cryptanalysis and intelligence in World War II, The Code Breakers, approached Rochefort in the late 1960s for information and assistance, but was declined upon the request of the director of naval intelligence, pp. 292-293.

Kimmel, Admiral Husband E., USN (USNA, 1904)
As commander in chief of the Pacific Fleet, possible choices he might have had if he had possessed prior knowledge of the probability of the Japanese attack on Pearl Harbor in 1941, pp. 71-72, 141, 160-161, 165.

King, Admiral Ernest J., USN (USNA, 1901)
As commander in chief of the U.S. fleet after the attack on Pearl Harbor requested estimation of future Japanese plans from Station Hypo in the spring of 1942, pp. 173-178; ignored recommendation of Distinguished Service Medal for Rochefort in 1942, pp. 250, 252, 257, 280.

Korean War
Fleet Evaluation Group, Pacific formed to investigate why U.S. was caught off guard by the North Korean attack in June of 1950, pp. 281-285; Central Intelligence Agency had intelligence regarding possible North Korean attack in mid-1950 but did not act on it, p. 300.

Kurita, Vice Admiral Takeo, IJN
Commander of first striking force at the Battle of Leyte Gulf in October of 1944; sent battle report about changing course which Rochefort offers as an example of the importance of careful translation, pp. 106-110.

Layton, Lieutenant Commander Edwin T., USN (USNA, 1924)
   As fleet intelligence officer in the early 1940s acted
   as a liaison between Rochefort and Admiral Nimitz in
   relaying Station Hypo's intelligence, pp. 145-148, 160,
   180-182, 184-185, 213; received daily Japanese ship plots
   from LT Holmes in the early 1940s, p. 180.

Leyte Gulf, Battle of
   VADM Takeo Kurita, IJN pulls out of the Gulf prematurely;
   had he stayed five minutes longer it would have meant
   disaster for ADM Kinkaid and the U.S. fleet in October
   of 1944, pp. 106-110; Japanese and American strategy
   studied at the Naval War College in the early 1950s,
   pp. 287-288; Rochefort's analysis of Admiral Kurita's
   strategy, pp. 287-289.

Macdonough, USS (DD-331)
   Commanding officers in the mid to late 1920s, pp. 49-50;
   operations with Destroyer Squadron 12 in the Pacific
   in the late 1920s, pp. 55-56.

McCormick, Captain Lynde E., USN (USNA, 1915)
   Rochefort's opinion of as war plans officer under Admiral
   Kimmel in the early 1940s, p. 209.

McMorris, Captain Charles H., USN (USNA, 1912)
   While on Nimitz's Pacific Ocean command staff spent time
   discussing intelligence with Rochefort in the early 1940s,
   p. 210.

Midway, Battle of (June 1942)
   Station Hypo's ploy to convince U.S. officers of Midway's
   identification in coded Japanese messages in early 1942,
   pp. 211-212; message of 25 May 1942 gave the United States
   precise information on planned Japanese attack, pp. 214-224,
   230-233; Army planes procured to patrol after battle
   by Admiral Nimitz, pp. 227-230; conflict between services
   over who could take credit for damage inflicted at Midway,
   p. 245; Japanese operations, pp. 248-250.

Morison, Rear Admiral Samuel E., USNR
   Not allowed in Station Hypo on advice of Admiral Nimitz's
   staff in the early 1940s, Rochefort's opinion that his
   15-volume History of the United States Naval Operations
   in World War II was a whitewash to defend the policies
   of the Roosevelt Administration, pp. 307-309.

Murphy, Captain Vincent R., USN (USNA, 1918)
   Planning officer of Nimitz's staff who resented Rochefort's
   unsolicited estimations of future Japanese operations
   offered in the spring of 1942, p. 176.

Naval Academy, U.S.
  Reaction of junior officer alumni to a non-academy officer (Rochefort) pp. 53-54.

Negat
  see Station Negat; Washington, D.C.

Nimitz, Admiral Chester W., USN (USNA, 1905)
  Appreciated need for strict security regarding U.S. codebreaking ability in the early 1940s, pp. 182-184, 232; visited Station Hypo in December of 1941, pp. 185-187; asked for Station Hypo's assessment of Japanese plans after he had already decided on a course of action in late spring of 1942, pp. 213-215, 244,, 301; met with Rochefort on 25 May 1942 concerning intelligence about Midway, pp. 217-224; handling of conditions on Oahu from December, 1941 to June, 1942, pp. 225-226; anecdote regarding the use of Army planes at Midway in exchange for control of carrier Saratoga's planes in mid-1942, pp. 227-230, 321-322; endorsed recommendation for Distinguished Service Medal for Rochefort in mid-1942, pp. 251-252; Rochefort felt he could have been supported by Nimitz to restrain his removal from Station Hypo in 1942, pp. 258, 262-263, 301-302; Rochefort praises foresight in accepting Station Hypo's Midway and Coral Sea intelligence, pp. 221-222, 301, 306-307; possible basis of selection by President Roosevelt to replace Admiral Kimmel as commander in chief of the Pacific in 1941, p. 321; Rochefort's assessment of his personality, pp. 322-323.

Pacific Strategic Intelligence Section (PSIS)
  Rochefort ordered to establish in the mid-1940s after pointing out need for study of Japanese capabilities before planned U.S. attack of country, pp. 271-272; accuracy of predictions generated by PSIS before end of war verified by U.S. Strategic Bombing Survey, pp. 272-273; organization in the mid-1940s, p. 274; conducted studies of Japanese war data for researchers, pp. 275-277; discovered variance between U.S. and Japanese recordings of the same events, p. 278.

Pearl Harbor, Hawaiian Islands
  U.S. preparations for war in the late 1930s, pp. 93-96; Station Hypo, pp. 97-99, 103-178; Rochefort's assessment of Japanese errors regarding 7 December 1941 attack, pp. 170-172; Admiral Standley's comment on the value of the attack, p. 172; second Japanese attack in February, 1942, pp. 203-208; conditions between 7 December 1941 and June of 1942, pp. 225-226; Joint Intelligence Center, Pacific Ocean Area, pp. 246, 256; U.S. inquiries into the attack of 1941, pp. 268-270; potential for air patrols prior to Japanese attacks, p. 165.

Pills
  No-doze type medications used to keep Station Hypo operating around the clock in the early 1940s, especially before the major engagements of World War II, pp. 124-125, 152.

Redman, Commander John R., USN (USNA, 1919)
  Washington-based cryptanalyst during World War II characterized by Rochefort as a glory-seeker, pp. 100, 166, 253, 294.

Reeves, Admiral Joseph M., USN (USNA, 1894)
  Commander, Battle Force in the mid-1930s who treated then-Lieutenant Rochefort as a protege and confidant, which he felt was more harmful than beneficial, pp. 82-84.

Rochefort, Captain Joseph J., USN
  Education, pp. 1-3; family, pp. 58, 62-63, 122-123, 261, 263-264; duty aboard oiler Cuyama (AO-3) in the early 1920s, pp. 3-5; engineering duty aboard destroyer Stansbury (DD-180) in the early 1920s, p. 5; watch and division officer aboard battleship Arizona (BB-39) in the mid-1920s, p. 5; Washington duty in Navy's budding cryptanalysis organization, 1925-1927, pp. 5-9, 14-22, 24, 26-32, 38-48, 58-59; executive officer of the destroyer Macdonough (DD-331), 1927-1929; studied Japanese while attached to the U.S. Embassy in Japan, 1929-1932, pp. 10, 36, 57-66, 75-76, 78-81; assistant operations officer aboard battleship USS California (BB-44) in the early 1930s, p. 52; on staff of commander, battle force and commander in chief of the U.S. fleet in the mid-1930s, pp. 55, 81-87; assistant district intelligence officer at San Pedro, 1936-1938, pp. 84, 87-91; navigator of the heavy cruiser New Orleans (CA-32), 1938-1939, pp. 89-92; staff of commander, scouting force, 1939-1941, pp. 92-97, 210; in charge of Station Hypo in Hawaii, 1941-1942, pp. 22-27, 98-178, 203-220, 265-266, 277, 307, 310; Rochefort's ability to be more than cryptology technician because of extensive U.S. fleet experience and knowledge of Japanese, pp. 144-151, 160-163; ordered to commander in chief of the Pacific staff as additional duty in 1942, p. 149; half-hour late for meeting with Admiral Nimitz to discuss Midway intelligence on 25 May 1942, pp. 217-224,, 230-233; second meeting with Nimitz and staff immediately after Midway battle where he is briefly commended for his part in the victory, pp. 227-230, 233-235, 243-245; commander, 14th Naval District recommends Rochefort for a Distinguished Service Medal, which is endorsed by Admiral Nimitz but ignored by Admiral King in mid-1942, pp. 250-252, 257, 280; sent dispatches with knowledge of Admiral Nimitz to Washington to segregate his activities from Station Negat in 1942, pp. 254-257; removed from Station Hypo in the fall of 1942 and temporarily ordered to command Intelligence Center, Pacific Operating, p. 256; ordered to Washington to work at Station Negat, which he refused to do,

October, 1942, pp. 258-261, 302-303; set up joint intelligence center in San Francisco in late 1942, pp. 263-264, 267-268; in charge of Pacific Strategic Intelligence Section in the mid-1940s, pp. 268, 270-279; ordered to command an attack transport after Japanese surrender in 1945 but brought back to Washington for senatorial inquiry into Pearl Harbor attack, pp. 268-270; brought out of retirement by orders to Fleet Evaluation Group, Pacific in mid-1950, pp. 281-285; requests return to retired list but asked to remain in Washington for varying tasks including translations for Naval War College, early 1950s, pp. 285-286; civic work after second retirement in March of 1953, pp. 289-290; advisor to movie in the mid-1960s, p. 291; requested by director of naval intelligence to refrain from discussing navy-related matters with interviewers, p. 292; negative view of medals and commendations, pp. 280-281, 234-235, 324.

Roosevelt, Franklin D.
As president in 1941, his role in bringing the United States into World War II, pp. 69-70, 77-78, 163-164.

Safford, Captain Laurance F., USN (USNA, 1916)
Set up Navy's cryptanalysis office in Washington in the mid-1920s and taught basics to Rochefort, pp. 6-8, 10-11, 21, 27; Rochefort's assessment of, pp. 12-13, 298; eased into less prominent position in naval communications operation at the outset of World War II, pp. 100-101, 252-253, 256; informal communications with Rochefort in the early 1940s regarding the strengthening of Station Hypo, pp. 98-100, 103, 140.

Saratoga, USS (CV-3)
Admiral Nimitz got the U.S. Army Air Corps to reluctantly allow their few remaining planes on Oahu to leave immediately for Midway in June of 1942 by promising them control of carrier Saratoga's planes during her upcoming stay at Pearl Harbor, neglecting to mention that she would only be in long enough to refuel, pp. 227-229; planes provided air protection for Honolulu in mid-1942, p. 230.

Spruance, Admiral Raymond A., USN (USNA, 1907)
Rochefort's opinion of his personality and comparison to Admiral Nimitz, pp. 322-323.

Standley, Admiral William H., USN (USNA, 1895)
Comment made in mid-December 1941 weighing value of loss of life at Pearl Harbor attack against unification of the United States, p. 172.

Station Bell(conner), Australia
Took over assistance role to Station Hypo in breaking Japanese codes after evacuation of Station Cast in the Philippines in 1942, pp. 143, 237, 313.

Station Cast; Cavite, The Philippines
   Working with Washington on Japanese naval code prior
   to the Pearl Harbor attack in 1941, pp. 114, 236; in
   assistance role to Station Hypo following attack on Pearl
   Harbor, pp. 119, 143.

Station Hypo; Pearl Harbor, Hawaiian Islands
   Personnel during the early 1940s, pp. 103-104, 110, 119,
   127, 151-152; job descriptions, pp. 104-105, 123, 128-129,
   152; inability to break Japanese code before Pearl Harbor
   attack in 1941, pp. 110-116, 158; condition of organization
   in the early 1940s and routing of information, pp. 112-113,
   152, 180-185, 188-191; facility in the early 1940s, pp.
   123-125, 127, 131-134, 153-156; use and importance of
   IBM machines, pp. 127-130, 157-158, 304; explanation
   of "red", "purple", "ultra", "magic", and other code
   names, pp. 135-139, 158-159; increased importance of
   station after 7 December 1941, pp. 116-117, 119, 140-145;
   possibility of averting disaster at Pearl Harbor had
   they been working on Japanese code instead of Washington,
   pp. 159-163; interpretation of Japan's changing code
   on 1 December 1941, pp. 168-170; estimation of future
   Japanese action requested by Admiral King in spring of
   1942; given first predictions of action at Midway and
   Coral Sea, pp. 173-178; frustration of information offered
   being treated skeptically or ignored in the early 1940s,
   pp. 203, 205-209, 211-212, 220; staff worked together
   to break Japanese operational order of 20 May 1942,
   pp. 215-218; security measures, pp. 154-155, 307, 310.

Station Negat, Washington, D.C.
   Shift of importance to Station Hypo after Japanese attack
   on Pearl Harbor in 1941, pp. 116-117, 119, 140-145; given
   credit by Admiral King for prior intelligence to Midway
   battle in 1942, pp. 251-252; gave Station Hypo trouble
   by attempting to exert control in the early 1940s,
   pp. 252-256.

Theobald, Rear Admiral Robert A., USN (USNA, 1907)
   As task force commander under commander in chief, Pacific
   in the early 1940s, advised by Nimitz of intelligence
   provided by Station Hypo, but ignored it, pp. 304-305.

Turner, Admiral Richmond K., USN (USNA, 1908)
   As task force commander in the early 1940s, when approached
   by a communications officer regarding intelligence bluntly
   dismissed any value, pp. 305-306.

United States Strategic Bombing Survey (USSBS)
   Team sent to Japan immediately following surrender in
   1945 to assess the extent of damage and its causes; able
   to advise Rochefort of the accuracy of his Pacific Strategic
   Intelligence Section's estimates during the latter part
   of the war, pp. 272-273.

World War II
   Prelude to the Japanese attack on Pearl Harbor in 1941, pp. 68-72, 75-78, 94; President Roosevelt's role in bringing the United States into the war, pp. 69-70, 77-78, 163-164; effect of events in Europe in the late 1930s and early 1940s on U.S. preparedness in the Pacific, pp. 70, 96-97, 112, 158; Battle of Leyte Gulf (October, 1944), pp. 106-109; Battle of Coral Sea (May 1942), pp. 174, 181, 189-190, 196-197, 237; Battle of Midway (June, 1942), pp. 175, 182, 189-190, 196-198, 214-224, 230-233, 237-240, 248-250; second Japanese attack on Pearl Harbor (February, 1942), pp. 203-208; Solomons campaign (August, 1942-February, 1943), pp. 240-242, 265; Guadalcanal campaign (August to November, 1942), pp. 240-242, 265, 300, 305-306; Rabaul (January, 1942), p. 315; Wake Island (December, 1941), pp. 317-318.

Yamamoto, Admiral Isoruku, IJN
   Conceived attack on Pearl Harbor in 1941, but from familiarity with U.S. Navy prior to the war knew Japan could not win in an extended conflict, pp. 67, 73-75; at the Battle of Midway, pp. 248-249; controversy over his death in 1943, pp. 313-314.

Yardley, Herbert O.
   Rochefort's negative assessment of cryptanalyst who claimed to be the first person able to break Japanese code in 1919, pp. 36-37, 40-41.

Zacharias, Rear Admiral Ellis M., USN (USNA, 1912)
   Japanese language officer in Rochefort's Washington operation in the mid-1920s who suggested him for language study duty in Japan in the late 1920s, pp. 58-60; as intelligence officer in World War II was not allowed into Station Hypo, p. 310; held theory that psychological warfare in the Pacific could have shortened the war, an idea that Rochefort discounts, pp. 309-311.

www.ingramcontent.com/pod-product-compliance
Lightning Source LLC
Chambersburg PA
CBHW080619170426
43209CB00007B/1464